I0422049

NOW THAT YOU ARE
Choirmaster

NOW THAT YOU ARE
Choirmaster

Soji Ojeniyi

Copyright © 2014 by Soji Ojeniyi.

ISBN: Softcover   978-1-4990-8668-3
             eBook   978-1-4990-8669-0

All rights reserved. No part of this book may be reproduced or transmitted in any form or by any means, electronic or mechanical, including photocopying, recording, or by any information storage and retrieval system, without permission in writing from the copyright owner.

Any people depicted in stock imagery provided by Thinkstock are models, and such images are being used for illustrative purposes only.
Certain stock imagery © Thinkstock.

Rev. date: 05/30/2014

To order additional copies of this book, contact:
Xlibris LLC
800-056-3182
www.Xlibrispublishing.co.uk
Orders@Xlibrispublishing.co.uk
616836

Contents

Other books by Soji Ojeniyi

Man Trust Thy Symphony

All in Africa

Star of Wonder

Live articles by Soji Ojeniyi available on *ezinearticles.com* include

Music the Stimulant
Lad Alone
The Pianist's Parkinson's
Death Dealt Deadly
Learning School

Follow the author

Facebook   Soji Ojeniyi
Twitter   @sojiojeniyi
Website   www.tinglescroll. org

Acknowledgment

I've worked with the strong and the weak. I've studied with masters and prodigies. I've performed with geniuses and irrationals. I still serve with the insignificant few and the relevant mass. I train the young and the aged. I direct the gifted and the ordinary.

I gleaned all within these pages from choirs of several denominations, schools, and communities through many years of plain old persistence and down-to-earth diligence. Their names and those of their good people have been altered for privacy reasons.

Specifically, I must thank my dad for the acoustic guitar he bought me when I was only four, which I never learnt to play, and for the electric organ that got into the house about five years afterwards, with which I later made my first attempt at Handel's *Messiah*. Lemi Ghariokwu gave me a toy piano as a prize at a reading competition that was held in our living room when I was only seven. Thank you, for with it, I taught myself tonality. My mum got me started on this reading habit. Thank you, for reading got me thinking I could write something someday. When I scribbled the first few pages of this book, my wife read it and thought it could fly. I thank Dr and Mrs F. F. Abudu for giving me a chance with a school choir that was quite a drill and a thrill. I thank Pastor Gideon Korede, who cared more about appreciating this book's prospects than understanding all it entails. Thank you for believing in me that much.

Now, I'm mighty grateful to all choirmasters who ever inspired me to greater heights without knowing they did: I thank my first role model, Wale the angel, who gave me my first chance at leading a choir; Dr Fagbemi, who gave me the first leadership opportunity at a non-denominational choir; Pius Hunyibo (of blessed memory), who only smiled the first time a priest invited me to his choir; David Adepoju, who made mass choir rehearsals seem so easy; and also everyone who tosses me a group of sweet-sounding voices or tone-deaf wannabes from time to time, even when I'm scared to death.

My heart won't stop beating the rhythm of gratitude to everyone at Author Solutions' Xlibris imprint who toiled to see this edition roll out of press, especially Chris Ablan, who laughed a little too much when he read the manuscript, and Ely Rivera, my senior publishing consultant, who has a unique understanding of authors with a one-pound drive and a one-dollar drag. Very many thanks to Randy Smith, Kay Benevades, Mary Lopez and Carla Cobar, who have all now become my friends.

Although inaccurate recounts and factual errors are mine alone, whether I have been lucky or rewarded with such rare experience as I seek to share, or whether I haven't, I'm indeed grateful to you all.

Soji Ojeniyi
May 2014

To David, world's grandest maestro

Intro

. . . .

If you have not worked effectively with a choir of one hundred voices, have not been equally effective with a choir of ten in a leadership position for not less than ten years, you need to read this book.

If you inherited a choir that is not quite in shape, whose music has no form, where rules are non-existent, and choristers are tone-deaf, please hurry and turn the pages.

I have been privileged to sing in, play in, and direct the worst, best, smallest, and largest of choirs with almost no tools at all to work with. I have seen the resistance of the naughty-natured and enjoyed the cooperation of the willing and obedient. I have seen choirs transformed in days with a total musical turnaround. In all these years, I have learnt fast and kept records.

I perused my notes and pored through reports generated from all my choir trainings nationally, honoured to turn the scorecards to you in singing words now that you are choirmaster.

THE CHOIRMASTER

The Place of Materials

. . . .

There's nothing worse in the experience of a choirmaster than having nothing to work on at the moment. If you ask around, you'll hear things from the ones who'll be sincere enough to tell you. Ask me what I did. I scheduled a prayer session out of passion, that's what! And that's terrible. When you have to convert your choir into a prayer squad, you have a crisis on your hands. Or you'll soon have one.

Get a picture of those who come to choir practice these days. They're not the overly pious. They constitute the excited ones, generally speaking. So don't you fool yourself into believing they'll enjoy the praying like you do. It bores them crazy. They don't want to pray. They came to sing, and sing you'll have to make them do.

What other thing do choirmasters do when they run dry? They write their own song and introduce it the same day. There you go. So many things wouldn't have been taken care of in this short time. The song would be too simple, too short. The harmony too weak, too cumbersome. The progression too absurd or absent. Now just imagine how he'd look, appearing before a forty-voice choir in this situation. If they belong to the city where I live, two-thirds of them won't attend the next choir practice. No one wants to sing an undone work, no matter the intention of the composer. Do all you want in your secret place and appear more than ready. That's when you're in good shape to lead. Knit the song together. Prune off the rough edges. Get the music flowing. Pull in the musicians ahead. Then work with your vocalists. Get to your choir with a done deal. They'll respond in tandem. Otherwise, you've got a raw show.

Anyway, let's discuss the things that help keep your choir's mill grinding through the year: *materials*. With materials, you have something on the music stand every week. They furnish you with the elements of preparation. So a wise choirmaster gets music literatures, music audios, and music videos. And to these he adds ample sheet music—from baroque oratorios to contemporary gospel scores. It's not the other way round (sheet music, then literatures and the rest). No! Literatures first; the others follow.

The literatures do two things: First, they inspire you; then, they round you up, broadening your scope of appreciation. By way of illustration, if you read the history of G. F. Handel before you begin work on the *Messiah*, at least two things happen to you instantly. First, you learn to make an independent but informed decision before you perform the work, just like every other conductor before you. You tend to feel not less than anyone who has ever performed the work in the last two and a half centuries, thereby assuming resoluteness. Second, you're inspired to write your own works, setting scriptures to music. These twin concepts—*education* and *inspiration*—are a crucial background resource in choir management. No choirmaster or choir mistress can afford to do without them.

Now, your choir has to do a song which borders on jazz, and you have perused literatures from which you gleaned the four elements of jazz—blue notes, syncopation, improvisation, and the uniqueness of altered timbre—then you are ready. You are ready to listen to the audio. Your mind is prepared to listen. The gates to your mind have a less rigorous job to do listening. You realise that observation is for the prepared mind. The man who has no idea what he wants to do stands in watch for nothing, for when his object of aim passes, he wouldn't even notice. You are better off, aren't you? You know when you hear what you've been waiting to hear. And you pin it down. You pause the disc player and encore that line over and over again, till you track it tight.

But don't even trouble yourself that much. Try this approach: listen to the audio once. (Preferably audio. Use video only as an instructional material for your vocalists or choir or just to inspire better stage performance.) Then play it back nineteen more times. Don't write anything the next nineteen times. Be sure to bathe your mind with the stuff. The first ten times help put you in the mind of the original creator of the work. The next ten times help put you in the mood. If you have a musical mind, about the twelfth or sixteenth time, you will have familiarised so well that you can follow the progression. If you really have talent, you will pick out the various timbres with a general appreciation of how they go to each cadence. At the minimum, you will pick the timbre of your own instrument as well as the part to which your voice belongs. Yet do not try to do much at this time. Just follow it to the end of the twentieth time. You'll then be ready to attempt scoring. Scoring means registering on paper what you have heard so far. Of course, you may play back some more times. The gist is, you must know it so well that you know it better than your choir.

A word of caution! Never ever listen for the purpose of copyright infringement. I'm about sure you understand copyright laws. One great sledge hammer on works of art in Africa and Asia today is piracy. But pirates are beginning to find that the gavel is heavier than the hammer. The law will catch up with them even in the weakest national judicial system. It's just a question of time. A people will evoke their own judiciary and evolve their own legality to the pinnacle of justice obtainable against the moneybags that cripple creativity, temporarily scaring genius off our continental shores.

All you need to do at the moment is sing what you have to sing on Sunday or Sabbath and get it over with without recording it. If you record, you may be tempted to sell to your congregation. Then you will have plugged into piracy. Let's walk out on that evil.

Realise that you can write your own songs and have music arranged for it. You may perform that in your church, record it whenever you want, and sell it to whomever you choose. It's your work. I recently heard about a young man who leads music in his church and got tempted to perform a gospel tune known all over the world with his name as author. The song was projected on the screen for the congregation to follow. Someone seated in the congregation that morning told me the story of how he had changed only a few words in the lyrics. The tune, progression, and vocal harmony were all left intact. This is nothing but pitiable poverty. He didn't even care that the majority of people in the congregation possibly have the discs right in their cars parked out in the church garage.

Neither did he know that if he had written his own song for that Sunday, he might have earned some respect for his name. So sorry a story. How shameless we have become.

But you don't want to do that. You don't want to temporarily steal someone else's work and demand applause even before you perform it under your name. That's what he did. If a man lacks the initiative, for pride, to give credit to the original owner of a work, he should learn then to keep his mouth shut rather than take the credit for himself unjustly and foolishly.

All right. We go to sheet music. Apart from buying them from stores, there are websites that post sheet music for free. Avail yourself of such opportunity. But never approach your choir with sheet music that you have not been through yourself. Spend time with the work. Get familiar with the parts. Pour through it from page to page like the conductor of an orchestra. Be certain you have a clear picture of what each part is going to do. Be absolutely explicit about the contrapuntal areas. When unclear, don't introduce the work yet. It can create confusion. You must be on hand for your part leaders. You can't afford to grope around while everybody is stuck. Don't forget that what makes you stand out as a leader is a clear-cut vision of the issues at hand and the issues to come. Never disappoint them.

To be sure, you can give yourself a rule: never introduce a piece you've not been through several times over the past two weeks. Remember that your choir ought to work on it for a minimum of two weeks before presenting it. You see, for music to be performed well, there must be much familiarity on the part of the performers. Even an improvisation need not be completely unfamiliar to the performer. At least you should have an idea about a few of the first phrases. Then you make up the rest. And when you are really 'posed', making up the rest won't be hard to do. In jazz, you will have had rehearsals, and your very improvisation would have been rehearsed too to ensure that you keep in the form. But choral music needs not all that rigour. All we advocate is that the choirmaster must really know the work he introduces. Otherwise, he doesn't qualify. Let no one get in the mental rut. If he can't, he can't.

Materials of the Place

•••••••••••••••

If you are choirmaster in a secular setting, your yoke is easy and your burden light. You don't need ten books on history of American religious revolution to sing a Negro spiritual. A rough idea may be sufficient for the leader of a school choir. Similarly, if you lead a community choir, you don't have to hold combined honours in sociology and anthropology to perform an SATB (soprano, alto, tenor, bass) arrangement of a folk tune.

But if you're choirmaster in a church, it is becoming of good conduct to appreciate the Bible and its contents. To that, you'll need to add other gospel accessories that help you understand the Word. These constitute the materials customary with the place where you perform. A translation of the Bible that suits you, in the language that you prefer, as well as a commentary, concordance, and Bible dictionary will definitely aid your ministry.

'But I'm not a pastor.'

'I know.'

'And I don't want to become one.'

'Fine.'

'So why do I need all 'em pastor things?'

'Think with me.'

Your choir has to perform Felix Mendelssohn's *Elijah*, a beauteous piece of oratorio. How on earth can you do justice if you haven't read the circumstances surrounding Elijah and the prophets of Baal? How do you add the action with which you may convert it into an opera? How do you communicate the message? Remember that music is an art. And an art is best rendered with background information.

Your day-to-day conduct in the church arena cannot possibly be anything close to what a choirmaster should be without close association with the Word. No one can imbibe an enviable Christian culture without a place in his or her heart for the materials of the place.

In my book *Man Trust Thy Symphony*, I endeavoured to give insight into how man is influenced by the things that go through the gates to his mind. That if man must take control of his bodily actions which are informed by his psyche's rumination, he must attempt—convenient or not—to first take control of materials with which his mind is bombarded from day to day. So you see, choosing to feed your mind with the Word results in living a comely life before God and before all. You will, almost naturally, behave well. Your life will be dignified because out of its issues will pour nuggets of high value.

You and I know the ills that have characterised the music department for too long. We must, therefore, be predetermined to avoid such a dirty lifestyle as may not edify the body of Christ. We want to walk worthy of our high calling. There's nothing greater than doing a song from a heart of purity. People will be blessed by purity more than by technicality. You may subscribe to the school that believes it is difficult to say which ought to be priority—purity or technicality. But you'll agree that it's not difficult to identify the three virulent evils that have plagued the music department for centuries—*verbal attacks, financial impropriety,* and *sexual indiscretion.*

They have weakened our vital wing of ministry, dragging what should otherwise be an easy thrust through the clouds to a blessed atmosphere of fellowship. You must endeavour to avoid them.

Hard as it may be, you must try to speak to and not talk at your choristers, especially if they're not on your payroll. They deserve some respect. You may give the toughest criticism and correct the most terrible offence they give through a careful choice of words. A joke sometimes does a better job than a scold. I get so easily displeased when someone's writing or doing something else while we have begun to sing. But I realise I have two options: I could talk down that person and make them feel less than human. The other option is better. I just say, 'Hey! Secretary to the Federal Government . . .' The person stops immediately, with a smile of course, especially if such a chorister does not fit the status of Secretary to the Federal Government. With a joke, you correct them more easily. You've heard it said that words are living things. The best choirmaster ranks among those who are able to keep their words in check. If you don't err in words, it's not likely you'll err in deed. Speak nicely to your people. Never ever arouse resentment. You are a leader, aren't you?

There's hardly any surer way to earn a choir's distrust than to mismanage the choir's funds, even if you didn't intend to or didn't do it at all. I'll share with you a story you don't want to know.

While in school, my best friend had just been elected treasurer of his department's association. We did our own laundry in those days and hung it outside to dry. The weekend after the election, my friend washed and hung his entire wardrobe out in the sun before he left for the academic arena to brush up on the week's workload. On his return, his clothes had found some more fun place to cool off for the weekend, never to return. To cut it short, resources were pooled so he could drop in town to acquire a couple of new clothes. When other members of the department noticed the change in this chic guy, they began to raise alarm. Now that got some dreadful laughs out of us, but it wasn't so funny. There was just nothing else for us to do.

Now you see why choristers see you in a new shirt, and they are sure with whose money you bought it, whether or not you can disprove it. The blackberry you have been using before you became choir mistress suddenly looks new. And then your purse. And on it goes.

The idea here is for you to be perceived as financially upright if you are financially upright. What you should do is delegate to someone better at bookkeeping. I didn't know jack about such things. So I just let the choir secretary do it. Do that instead of being choirmaster, financial secretary, and treasurer at the same time you play an auditor. Just deal with someone you trust, and devote the rest of your attention to the music.

The issue of sexual stupidity will be discussed later.

Professionalism of Measure

●●●●●●●●●●●●●●

A twelve-week training programme a few years ago ran me into something funny. In that choir, like many others in this part of the world, there was a craze for titles rather than a care for essence. Have you ever seen a choir with a choirmaster who is different from the choir leader, who is not the same person as the choir coordinator, who again is separate from the choir director, who holds a different office from the music director? Of course, there was no choir; otherwise, my services would not have been required. Yet they had many other titles: secretary, treasurer, financial secretary, assistant this, assistant that, and so on.

Now, you and I know that you don't need to have all that to run an effective choir. And if you must have so many offices where the choir is large, why don't you rather have functional music offices? What did I do? Exactly that! I dissolved all their offices, chose one of the few dedicated choristers as secretary to assist me with paperwork, and I directed the music. Even now, when I look back, I still wonder why practically everyone should have a title and almost all do nothing. There were even truants who had big titles. They ran back when they heard about what we were doing. Some of them couldn't fit in for long. Many couldn't fit in at all.

The success or failure of a choir, I need not say, rests with its leader. It depends on how much he understands and puts into effect the subsets of choir management: *passion, knowledge,* and *discipline.*

I served in the music department of a church for ten years. I took over from a man who lacked any form of passion. He couldn't learn to sing a four-line chorus without a hitch. He didn't always make it to choir practice early, and he saw nothing particularly wrong with it. Worse still, he never prepared for the rehearsal.

Don't get me wrong. I love and respect this man very much, and he knows. He has a great passion for his field of study. He is notable all over town. But music—church music—that's not where his passion lay. He wasn't doing wrong intentionally. He just didn't belong there. When I took baton, it was *only* passion (I'm ashamed to say) that led me on for some time.

So what is passion? *It is a burning desire that ties a person enthusiastically to a thing without time limit. It is not motivated by reward but by fulfilment. Joyful satisfaction feeds it full.*

There is, however, no substitute for cognate knowledge. While in the university, I went to fellowship and joined the choir. One time, the choir got a lady to lead it who was passionate but ignorant. You know the kind of sister who sings so well, she's the only one who gets blessed. She could sing but couldn't make anybody else do anything. We patched up through those two long semesters.

But the person who loves what she's doing and knows about it is different. Do not be the choir mistress who knows no rudiments of music but is bustling and boasting about her post. You need knowledge very much, and you need very much knowledge.

Discipline is where the greatest problem is. Passion is fine. Knowledge is good. But indiscipline would inevitably destroy them both. You need self-discipline and institutional discipline. The former for yourself, the latter for your choir. You need it in three areas: time, body, and words.

There must be a starting time and a closing time. You ought to obey it and enforce others to obey it. Tell them they can't be one minute late. Once, I had the wife of a top church council official in my choir. She came late one evening by less than two minutes, and I sent her back home.

We have already been through words and the importance of keeping them in check so that a leader does not err so easily in them.

The following—musical passion, cognate knowledge, and overall chorale discipline—constitute the principles of choir management for the intending professional who measures up to maturity. Major in these, and you may well minor in the rest.

'Are you telling me to delegate certain functions?'

'Of course, dear.'

Delegation is key to effectiveness. Let someone else do the other things that do not border on critical control points.

Say you have selected the piece for the next choir practice. You are busy with other things like your daily work schedule or the rigors of academic deadlines. Then get someone in your choir to run the fifty copies you need ready for the next rehearsal.

You are planning a concert. You have selected the numbers. You are now writing the lines for the musicians to play. Then let someone write the letters and mail them to your invitees. Let her design the cards and book the hall. Keep your mind where it should be—the music. Give them a push whenever they need it. But never let anything be so important to you enough that it takes your attention away from the music. Measure your energy. Harness it and channel it aright.

*   *   *

What better measure do you have of how professional you have become without an attempt at something lofty? Your choir stays awake and in shape when there is something to look forward to. So give them a focus. Plan a programme—a musical one—to the exclusion of all else.

It's their day or their night. There must be a major performance in view. If they'll never have time to prepare, collect all the songs you've performed weekly over a season and select the best pieces so far—normally their favourites. Schedule a night and perform all of them. There must be a special event for your choir. Remember, professionalism is measured in performance.

A Measure of Professionalism

• • • • • • • • • • • • • •

Just about a year ago, I was asked to speak to the choir of a church that was younger than its age. My hostess had briefed me about the urgency of this need and the need to keep my speech within my profession since I wasn't the only speaker scheduled. (That's another way to say 'You had better not speak like a pastor.' So I made a note of it.) In the short time I had, I endeavoured to reiterate, among other things, that there are three important factors that make a choir tick. Number one, *music*. Number two, *music*. Number three, *music*.

So the emphasis of any choirmaster must be the music. And you only command respect when you get on the path of professionalism by adding knowledge to your passion. You should train on an instrument or two. The more familiar you get with a musical instrument, the better you get with your choir. Get your feet to a school of music and let your heart go with you. Learn and practice daily. You'll be glad you did.

Do not stop there. Attempt certification.

'Now you cross a line,' you say.

'Yeah! But it's a good line.'

'I don't want to be some music teacher, man!' you scream.

'I know.'

'So why do I need an exam, a certificate, and all that trash?' You're hurting.

'Because you are a choirmaster now. And not just a trader, an engineer, and a factory worker put together.'

Let's get serious. Nothing will happen in your choir until you have shot above the pack. They'll never get better until you get better. You see differently from the day you walk through the door to sit a music exam, even if it's only in Theory of Music. And that's all I advocate—Theory of Music. You may train for violin. But you don't have to sit a violin exam. Take your piano classes. But you don't have to sit a piano exam. So much comes with taking an instrument exam in music. But for general appreciation, a theory exam would suffice. It will put you on a platform where you may consider institutionalising your choir. And what do you think makes a choir strong and eternally relevant? Institutionalisation, of course! That's the place every choir needs to go. And that's the place every choir would not go. And the latter's why many choirs would never go far. You should, therefore, go for the standard, at least, even if the whole world goes for less.

Don't be fooled. As you read this, over half a million people already sat or are preparing to sit music examinations this year alone. My worry is: why are 'leaders' the only ones who wouldn't do the right things? These are people from all known and unknown and lost and forgotten corners of the world, aiming and striving for some professional qualification in the same field in which you have been called to lead. Why on earth should you sit around going once or twice to prepare a meek singing group of local champions? You should do better than that. If you have an opportunity to qualify, you should while it is still available. Like the president of a nation, you have one great opportunity to lead your people to a better place than where you met them.

'But I didn't campaign to be choirmaster.'

'Neither did Moses to lead the Israelites.'

'Presidents don't go to school while in the White House.'

'Then you are luckier than a president if you are right.'

The last time I checked, the first gift a president gets after winning an election is a security briefing. Didn't they tell you that at Yale? From what I gather, that's tougher than going to school.

'I'm not president. Don't kid me, SOJ.'

'Neither was David in the court of Saul nor Asaph in the palace of David. Neither is Zukerman before the Philharmonic nor Walter before the Walter Thompson Orchestra.'

You should move close by some measure from time to time to professionalism. Yet you should move further. Add to your theory and practice an 'audiencial' *experience*. Go to a concert given by art musicians. See how things are professionally done. Well, don't just sit in the audience ticking off the tunes on your programme booklet. You are not there for a bag of popcorn at intermission. You are a choirmaster, aren't you? So, your concern would begin with orchestra warming. Then the curtain-raiser. What happens to the ambience? How cleanly, crisply, and noiselessly is the sound managed? How marvellous is the stage set? How many musicians constitute each part? How organised is the choir stand? What instruments make up each section? What is the peculiarity of the composers whose works are performed? Which conductor expresses your perceived moods of the works best? What would you have done differently if you were privileged to direct this choir or conduct this orchestra?

Now you see why it's cool to move pretty close to professionalism. Each of your moves measures you closer to the place where you should be.

If you have need of guidance with respect to which training and/or certification you should take, please reach me through sojiojeniyi@gmail. com. I would be pleased to give such advice free of charge. Remember to put *Now That You Are Choirmaster: guidance* in your subject line.

THE CHOIR

Records

. . . .

What do you expect your choir to look like five years from now? Most likely, such an idea is not crystallised in black and white yet. Well, let's rearrange the picture so that you are still choirmaster in five years' time, and you have the opportunity to look back from that vantage point. In that case, can you give an account, if only in highlights, of what you've taken the choir through in the past five years? If you were to hand over the choir to a new choirmaster this evening, do you have anything to give over, such as achievements, challenges, what to watch out for, and so on?

When I run choir trainings for ten weeks, say, I ensure that at the end of the day, I'm able to deliver a report of what went on during our time together. Now that is not so easy to do when you consider that I'm doing so many things together. Most of such trainings are tailored to the needs of the choir in question. So in some cases, I'm preparing voices for the weekly performance and special events. At the same time, I'm giving a musicianship class on instruments and monitoring progress. In the same period, I'm drilling vocalists on 'the tricks' that make the feel. Yet we have a choir management class running for leadership. And so on. Many times, this gulps several hours a week. Keep in mind that I'll still give several other classes outside that setting every week, sometimes every day. Don't forget that I may get a speaking engagement, for which I need a lot of time to prepare. And if I have a writing project going, I'll have to be at my desk daily. Hold fast the rigors of 'keeping in shape'. And then family. And then . . . Well, after all these, I'll still deliver an accurate account of what's done.

My point is, you must endeavour to keep records: records of attendance in rehearsal and performance; records of music performed when and for what; records of finances, if it ever concerns your choir; records of uniform, especially if you have more than one—the making, the dry cleaning, etc. Records are vital, for they eventually form your choir's history. And which choir shouldn't have a history? Even if you have a small group, you still need records. Who is in this or that part? What is in your library? Write it all down and put a date to it. Apart from each chorister's song file, a choirmaster must open a file of songsheets for the choir. This should never head in a third direction: it's either in the library or in choir practice.

'What on earth do I do with that?'

'Give it over to the person who takes over from you.'

Except you expect to be choirmaster forever, you need to generate materials for the next head. Put things down and annotate appropriately. Several years down the line, the world will be glad you did.

'Now, you gimme too much. I don't think I wanna be no choirmaster no more.'

'Please, be. Your country needs you.'

And it's no hard to do. Delegate! All you have to do is do all you can and must. Give over what you don't have to do. Someone will be glad to do it. There's always a Bidden, a Gore, and a loyal Sambo. Raise an assistant. Be sure she is strong where you are weak. You are strong in organising. She is strong in details. You don't like details. Let her do it. You'd rather run the performance. She's comfortable with bookkeeping. She'll be glad to help. After all, it's what she likes to do. People will help you if only you'd ask respectfully. Just quit thinking they are all dumb. They may not know what you know. But they might know what you don't know. They are great people. Your choir runs because they are there. Imagine a strike action. You won't be the choir all by yourself. You are choirmaster because there is a choir. They deserve respect. Sometimes, I spend a couple of minutes telling them how wonderful they are.

Remember, record keeping doesn't have to be cumbersome. Sometimes, all you need is a table of three columns. Label each as necessary. Then enter your records per time.

Performance

. . . .

Chorale music is a message. Therefore, it is important to *plan* everything and time it to the second from the moment you are introduced to when you get done. At the minimum, get a general idea about how long your song would take. Then schedule approximately one and a half minutes around it. These days, no one can cope with a conductor walking around after his choir has been called. Be sure, for example, that all your microphones are set before you are called up. Parley with the soundman. Spare the house anything other than your music. The very words you speak, if any, should have been carefully chosen, with nothing repeated. Your voice-over should have been painstakingly rehearsed as part of the music. Each stroke and signal of the conductor must be understood and executed. Every pass must be honoured and observed. No misses. No extra note. No extra beat. Avoid extras as though they were a plague. You make it or break it right there as you perform.

But all these do not happen by chance. The only way to the confidence that conveys an excellent performance is *preparation*. You must take the time and effort to adequately prepare, approaching each rehearsal as though it were a real performance. Otherwise, you are not at home before a congregation. So run each part until you are sure it's tight. Once you have taught the song, listen to each part and then all parts. Fuse it with the music. Ensure a blend. Your ears must pick the slightest off-norm. Correct it right there. Make them do the right one over and over again, overwriting the wrong. Realise that if your choir goes home with the wrong thing, you may never be able to correct it. So correct it at once.

See to it, however, that you do not over-drill them. Make them learn what they can at a time. Oftentimes, you'll find that their attitude to a new song is not so warm. Let them live with the song for some time then. Except your choristers are very well trained, it's unlikely they'll jump at a new piece the first time it's introduced. You'll see that your plan takes shape in preparation. Your preparation is portrayed in rehearsal. But your performance is in *delivery*.

Project your preparation to *delivery*. Learn, therefore, the art of delivery and be certain that it begins with body language, unto your filing upstage, the actual singing—with which come pronunciation, articulation, gesticulation, tune rendition, and facial expression. Everything counts. Discourage the conflict that usually occurs between the message in the music and the expression of the music. If there's 'joy like a river' in your song, your choir shouldn't run like a worried dripping tap.

'SOJ, are you saying I should psyche them up?'

'I'm saying do more than that!'

If you are tense, they'll be tense. If you're light and full and free, that's exactly how they'll be. Give your lead vocalist a cup of coffee before she goes up. Buy her a bottle of Coke after she comes through. If your choir is really a choir, they'll be as excited at a wedding as they would at a funeral. So smile at them before you begin to conduct. They'll smile back. *Morale: A smile is contagious.*

They have just done the first line of the refrain correctly. My friend, they moved a mountain. What should you do? Give them Uncle Sam's finger! Or you just got a stroke of the glottis syncopated. What should you do? Hang your baton on your right ear and give them a double thumbs up!

*   *   *

When they are well-groomed and properly clad, they exude a brilliance that commands the sights. As much as I advise an utmost regard for modesty, set the affordable appearance that suits your choir. If you must concentrate on the music, put somebody in charge of that. Should you have little respect for your choir, you can only hope to expect the same from an audience. Help the brothers give up baggy trousers, if it's not costume. Scope the sisters to give up shapeless skirts, if it's not comedy. Bulging purses may stay on the seats until after the singing. Discourage unkempt hair and dusty shoes. Your audience is your jury. An impeccable finish or you're finished! Would you rather have them hasten a verdict: the music which we are about to listen to is as discordantly sloppy as the looks of its performers?

Acquiring a uniform for your choir need not require a UN peacekeeping mission. A few years ago, I was invited to prepare a choir for a concert. Let's call it Four Corners Church. We scheduled several rehearsals over weeks. We drilled and pruned and rounded rough edges. I scored the music and brought in musicians from my band. We married the voices with the music, and everything was splendid. On the night of the occasion, however, two-fifths of the choristers didn't show up. I kind of shoved the choir mistress aside.

'What's going on?'

'They didn't buy their suits,' she said.

I felt I had been dealt a terrible blow. Can you imagine dark-coloured suits in a dimly lit and poorly ventilated building under a tropical climate? The lady just wanted to wear a suit. But she could have worn it all by herself. She could afford it. But many of the choristers were students, full-time housewives, petit traders, or something in between.

You don't have to compel anyone to buy anything just to qualify to sing in concert. We all love the experience of travelling abroad shopping for what suits our choristers best. I've done this before. But it may not fit the situation of your choir at this time. There are many alternatives at your disposal. One, choose a uniform that is affordable. Two, dictate a colour for dress code. Three, use your robe or one of your ceremonial uniforms. You could even set one apart for a long time before the event. Four, combine pieces of two or three uniforms. Matching pieces of uniforms may be combined to look completely new. Or each part may use a different uniform or colour, provided it matches with what the others are wearing. Five, let those who can afford to buy the new agreed uniform buy for one or two others also. Six, find partners in the congregation to help fund the uniform. In fact, the entire programme may be funded this way. There are people in church who love and believe in what you are doing.

We had this Christmas carol a few years ago. Let's call it Saved Christian Church. I was so carried away with the music, I didn't remember that any uniform was necessary. When it was about two weeks to go, a woman called me and asked, 'What do you folks intend to wear?'

I said something that must have sounded like this. 'We, ah . . . we, ah . . . we have nothing in mind, ma'am.'

Knowing who I am (the ole boy who worries about nothing other than the music), she scheduled an appointment with the choir immediately. She sent in a tailor and bundles of materials, like an angel, you know. It was like I was watching a movie. I put someone in charge to make sure that everyone present or absent that night got on the tailor's list, per size. The following week, the uniforms were waiting, all labelled. My choir was ecstatic. I grouped the numbers and dictated another code to match the traditional tunes. That added more colour. Everything was timed and perfectly organised. I can never forget that night. Neither can I forget the woman angel. Sometimes, when I remember that night, I smile. Right now as I write, I'm moved to tears. Such is what can happen if you don't burden people unnecessarily. (But don't forget the uniform like I did.)

Acquiring a uniform for your choir is easier than maintaining it. Again, you may have to delegate, especially if you have a system where everyone submits his or her uniform after use. This is the case where the choir uses a robe, for obvious reasons. Contract a dry cleaner and have them packed away in polythene jackets. If choristers keep their own uniforms, advise similar laundry treatments and subsequent consecration.

Why on earth should I bother about your choir robes? Trust me. I once drilled a choir in Victoria Island for a concert and completely forgot about the robes, only to be called into the Head of School's office one afternoon before the event. And oh how she yelled in bewilderment!

'For God's sake, the concert is tomorrow night!'

I could only stare, stunned!

Well, the choir robes had been locked somewhere since the darling business manager couldn't disburse funds for dry-cleaning. Of course, the buck that passed between the business office and sanitation department headed towards a more expensive dry-cleaning outfit which runs a twelve-hour service. We were lucky to pick up the robes four hours before the concert. *Morale: Delegate but follow up.*

*   *   *

From time to time, when I work with a choir, people ask me about what to eat and what not to drink. Wherever they got those rules from, you never can tell. Recently also, I was teaching a history class in a renowned college of music. A student raised his hand and asked a question about his friend's voice that reacts to some toothpaste. May we lay all these things to rest here?

The best advice is to get familiar with your voice. You will get familiar by use, of course. But many would still not be satisfied. So let's take some further guidelines.

Temperature has a sure influence on the voice. If you live in temperate climate, you probably already know that voice rehearsals are hardly scheduled before noon. You'd rather wait for the sun to rise, warming the air that goes through your larynx. You see, the vocal cords are cords indeed—strings, if you please. Like all string instruments, the cords vibrate better for sound production when warm rather than when cool. So you should prefer a warm drink to a cold one when you are about to perform. Why else do you think the green room is warmer than the stage? To precondition the voice, of course. You don't want to eat anything below 30°C. Where a hot meal is not your style, let the meal wait until after your performance or eat it a lot earlier so you can allow your cords to warm up afterwards. Please understand that heat as a by-product of the body's metabolism should serve as leverage for the singer.

Dry grits and all coarse food particles may cluster around your larynx. They are potent enough to ruin a solo performance if they get on the vocal cords. So you want to allow the children to enjoy those tempting popcorn and peanuts for the night. Grab the popcorn bag when you have no performance in view.

I understand that some solo artistes cut down on oily foods for their career. This is good discipline. But if your oily food is warm enough, I don't foresee a problem. Take a bite! And another. And yet another.

If you have any allergies, you may wish to consult your physician. I want to suggest that anything harsh on inhalation should be avoided, especially aerosols like insecticides and pesticides. But if you have eaten or drunk anything to which your voice reacted, you may have an allergy on your hands. Please, see your doctor to be sure.

*   *   *

In performance, there's something almost as important as your music: the quality of *sound* that is crisp, clear, rich, and full. It deserves your respect no less than the chief of staff deserves the respect he earns from the first citizen. Of course, you know that if the president shows up anywhere, does anything, hires or fires anyone for any task or any reason, that appearance, that piece of assignment, that appointment or that decision has passed through the careful eyes, critical mind, and scrupulous judgement of his chief of staff. That is why this right-hand man is selected, never elected, with utmost care.

You must, therefore, learn to *select* the *sound* that delivers your music with an equal amount of caution. The best performers of all time give not less than an hour to soundcheck for a two-hour performance. The best of the best music directors hire a sound manager to whom is given a broad latitude of clout so that his operation is in no way impeded by anyone whose thought pattern and process are pitiably less sophisticated than this precious promise of a profound performance. Sound engineering companies now undertake the task of providing befitting sound at the topmost quality humanly possible over a two-week period to world-class musical concerts that hold in just one night.

Learn your lesson now. Dishonour sound at your own peril! Realise that I did not write: dishonour sound at the peril of your music. No! At your own peril! Reason is, for those of us who perform, performance is an end in itself. Whenever it's not done fine, something dies within us. Never ever treat it with levity.

I remember taking four hours to sequence a soundtrack, two hours to prep the choir to do only a few lines of chorus, then an entire hour adjusting the sound that the sound men had worked at very well already. The sound room in that auditorium was up in the back without monitors. So I kept going back and forth, up and down the stairs, to get what I wanted. You see, it can't be well enough when it's not good enough. This performance I now write about was done in honour of my then choir's matron—a woman whose hair had gone gray with the passing of fifty harmattans. When that soundtrack hit the air waves blended with exquisite voices enhanced by superior sound technology, the auditorium came alive, and the memory of it never faded from the minds of those who were there. When your sound is well, the ambience booms well, and an aura of wellness encapsulates you.

A few plays have flowed through my pen. As of the writing of this book, only one has been published. When *Star of Wonder* premiered, everything that everybody had done in preparation was almost entirely marred by poor sound management. A director had been hired for the work, so the business of sound was taken out of my hands. I couldn't even get a keenly interested actress into the cast. My assignment was strictly to work the choir and vocalists. I worked with a seasoned pianist. Drummers had tough schedules with dancers. The director faced actors and actresses. We all toiled away at the expense of sound. We ran the dress rehearsals but were unable to bring the soundmen into it. On the evening of the performance, with about three-quarters of a thousand elites packed in the audience under a single giant tent, watching a 13,000-dollar performance go down the drain, I recall the director saying, 'When a show has become like this, all I can do is watch.' I felt sorry for him. That was the last show he got signed to direct in that institution. He could simply have convinced the producer he needed sound set up for the dress rehearsals. That he failed to do at his own peril.

How may you find minimum guidance when it comes to sound management? First, the *equipment*. Microphones pick up sound signals. The signals go through a mixer and/or equaliser (for fine processing) to an amplifier which boosts it out to the speakers. (Sometimes, the speakers are managed using a separate device in place of traditional equalisers, in addition to the amplifiers and mixer.) There are usually several lines (of microphones and other tone-generating instruments, e.g. keyboards, guitars, violins, drum pick-ups, etc.) running into the mixer so that all sound is processed from a single unit. (At least that's what happens in many cases.) You only have to plug in microphones etc. to the mixer. The mixer is plugged to the amplifier. Speakers are connected to the amplifier as an outlet per line the same way mixer lines are connected to the amplifier. It's a chain of *generation* (microphones) to *production* (speakers). In between these are the *processor* (mixer) and *booster* (amplifier).

Second, *how it all works*. It actually depends on the venue, its content, and the purpose. Organising sound for a fifty-folk indoor event with furniture and high ceilings is entirely different from planning sound for an outdoor programme in front of 20,000 people. Putting sound together for a concert with an audience of 500 is very much different from working sound for a meeting to be attended by thirty seniors. For a choir mistress's purpose, let's assume that you only have about a hundred people in a little hall about a hundred and fifty square feet or so. We must also assume that the pieces of your equipment were chosen by someone who knows a thing or two about such stuff, in which case *they agree*.

The simplest thing to do is position your speakers aright. This can mean the difference between beauteous sound production and horrible feedbacks plus distortions. They, including monitors, should be positioned so that they face away from the microphones in a fundamental sound setting. You see, just basic stuff. Yet people do weird things. I'll save you a story and carry on with the advice.

Another thing you can do before and during a meeting is, adjust all knobs on the mixer to satisfaction. It's not rocket science. It can be done by you if your ears work right, and I think they do, or you wouldn't be choirmaster. They are just potentiometers. If you ever raised the volume of your radio set, you can do this. These days, you even do much more than that. You adjust the volume of your mobile phone mp3 player, don't you? A potentiometer is just a device that regulates the inflow of voltage into a (usually an audio) device.

On the mixer, there are several of them lined up against each channel, right? Right! There you are. They are all labelled. You don't have to know everything. But a few of them should concern you greatly. With them under your control, your life is easier. Without them, you may be rudely shocked. They are *Gain, High, Mid, Low, Reverb,* and *Pan.* I'll use layman language so we can take out too much technicality and still make meaning to you.

With *Gain,* you can raise or lower the volume of that particular channel.

With *High,* you can alter its high frequency range, that is, the range captured by twitters.

With *Mid,* you can increase or decrease the mic's sound pull.

With *Low,* you get to raise or reduce the loudness of the low frequency range of sound, that is, the bass effect.

Reverb is short for reverberation, what you call echo effect. Play with it depending on your need. A person making a speech does not need much of this.

What's left is *pan.* This helps you redirect (or restrict) the output of a channel to a speaker. This way, a microphone (or any device) gets louder on one speaker (wing) while it's softer on the other.

In a nutshell, *planning* in detail, *preparing* carefully, an excellent *delivery,* a comely *appearance, voices* in good order, and a stately *soundcheck* are the six sine-qua-non vertices of a star performance.

The Naughty-Natured

. . . .

Not everyone is lucky every time to have a choir of pure-bred saints. As though plagued by a strange kind of liberalism corrupted by an estranged mixed-multitudism, one finds that there are a few, if not a handful, of really naughty ones. Keep in mind that we have raised a generation of people who are not used to rules. A crop of people who seem to defy every set standard, doing what they please, when they please, how they please, constitutes a large part of the group we usually have. That is their only realm of existence. They just can't help it. They are the ones who are never punctual. They'll rather put on something a little different from the uniform. They leave their shirts loose while everybody else tucks theirs in. What do they have to say? 'It's a fitted shirt.' They know so much fashion and so little else. They would sit together when they don't belong in the same part. One of them would pick up a chair and raise it over his head to show he is very excited during praises, while the other would whistle during the message to show she's really getting blessed! One would restring his guitar upside down for a show of iconoclasm, while the other would place her right hand above the left on the saxophone for a show of specialty. They'll turn up their cuffs (and not roll it up). They'll overgrow their fingernails and insist on playing the piano despite a lack of precision. They'll talk back while the choir mistress talks, differing on everything. They'll form a naughty party, for the purpose of mischief. Their make-up would be worn too loud. Their mobile phones would ring too many times in every choir practice. They'll sit awkwardly and frown throughout. They'll not sing because their notes are 'too high'. They are the vocalists who switch off their microphone and tell you it's not working. (They are unsure how their voices would sound.) These people have a consistent disregard for everything that is good, fitting, and proper. You may have some other weird ones in your choir, but let's stop here.

Honey, there are no hard and fast rules in dealing with these naughty people. But deal with them you will! Or you won't have a choir very long. Or you won't be choirmaster very long. Or you won't enjoy your time as choirmaster. Or all three! And you ought to enjoy whatever it is you are doing. When a choir is properly institutionalised, the burden lightens. Don't fantasise; it doesn't ever varnish. By institutionalisation, I mean there must be an entrance format. There should also be a modus operandi guiding the day-to-day running of the house. There should be a time to arrive and to leave. There should be specific things that'll be done per time. In fact, I've found that when you have your choir time planned out in strict schedule, there's little time for nonsense. If there's none at the moment, sketch a constitution that guides the house and edit it from time to time. Get a copy ready for sighting, at least, by each person at the point of admission.

However, you can't screen off every trouble this way. Well, you don't have to live with day-to-day worries about what trouble is coming and from whom it is coming. If you do, you'll have one problem too often. Yet if you're working hard and smart, you may have a crisis every once in a while. This is normal in any gathering of humans. Otherwise, you have dummies.

But some people are just a pain in the neck. For these, early on your assumption of duty, establish firmness. Not harshness. Just strictly and firmly say 'no' to some things that you are sure would be a clog in the choir's wheel. And say why. Where a person is unreasonable, take him up and deal with him in a manner consistent with your choir's constitution. And please, do things formally. Remember the power of the printed matter. Keep in mind that all you want is discipline. So don't take things too far. As soon as you achieve it, make the culprit your best friend.

Once, I got this invitation to prepare a choir—no! Two choirs—within four days. I don't get this kind of invitation every day. I suppose the same is true with many people. When I got mine, it wasn't framed that scary. It was an Assemblage of God (let's call it that). By the first evening, when I got there, I met a scarier scenario. I'll share with you since we are now friends.

The entire church had been converted into a choir—everyone who could open their throat to sing something out—the previous Sunday. My job now was to train this entire group of raw humans in four evenings. Among them were people probably my father's age. The house would then split into two groups afterwards to rehearse whatever I would have taught them and render it in a competitive setting two weeks later. What all this actually meant was that I would get involved in some choir administration instead of just music. Good golly! I had better get to work. That is exactly what I did. I began with auditioning and spent the whole of the first evening doing that.

Naturally, I ran into a naughty-natured lady who just didn't want to audition. Eventually, when she did, she qualified for soprano. And then began an argument about why she thought singing alto was better for her since she 'shouldn't just get to sing the soprano' that I 'thought' she should sing. You probably know what I did. I just smiled, ignored her, and went on with the others. We were friends throughout my four funny flights of nights.

Sometimes, you don't even need to go far at all. Ignoring certain people after a verdict can do the trick. Again, apply some discretion, and do all that must be done to achieve a better-than-sane environment almost all the time.

But then, we may think what we want. The naughtiest chorister behaves in a way that seems fine to him. If we understand this, we will see that some do not mean any evil for doing what they do. Such can be moulded to fit into the choir's environment. For example, if a person has needs for a position of authority, he might exhibit such traits not necessarily because he seeks your downfall. At such times, it is good to listen. That person may just have a good idea. He only sounds repulsive. He has nothing whatsoever against the colour of your skin. He only wants to make a contribution to the choir's development. Hear him out. Then make him a friend. Give him a responsibility again and again to execute. Let him report to you personally. Then, he learns that the buck stops at your desk. Let not your mind be preoccupied with danger at your sighting him, or dangerous he will become but only to you. You are the head. Walk tall and fearless. Love all, but take no nonsense. Help them see function as priority over titles.

Be careful when you introduce something that's completely new. This might arouse resentment. People don't always want their boats rocked. Therefore, introduce new concepts and new songs with a touch of the familiar. This way, they are comfortable. If they are used to ballad, then do not suddenly bring in rap, kicking out the ballad. Only add a few lines of rap for now. Add it in the language with which they are at ease. They'll be smiling from ear to ear. They'll receive a thunderous applause from the congregation (if your congregation is allowed to clap). You'll have a nice time. In the same vein, add your dissonant experiments to their familiar consonance. This is the way to a happy choir.

You will reduce the possibility of friction if you cast the air of success when your choir meets rather than the clouds of doubt. They need to feel that their performance will succeed. Then they will repel you less. If they think more of succeeding and less of avoiding a flop, they take a liking to you more easily. This is quite easy to elicit if you begin from your very first day before them. The generality of them will generalise about you this first day. It is called a first impression. If they think you can perform, you've made it. If they doubt your leadership that first day, it will take quite some time to make up for it. So get your materials together, having rehearsed thoroughly, and enjoy yourself while you treat them to a brief speech. Then begin the warm-up exercises and launch the singing properly. That's why they came.

And if you know another reason why they came, then consider it. I'll lend you one because you bought this book. Try it. Some very young people might be in your choir who have no idea what to do with their lives. Sow in them some idea from your informed, privileged position. Prepare a two-minute career talk by next Saturday (or whenever else is your next choir practice). Do the speech ahead of the singing. Be careful not to get longer than a minute or two. They have heard that many people who have been in the choir make it in life. (Daddy and Mummy think so.) Make it juicy. Make it fine. Launch your singing immediately afterwards. (They have to associate your care with the music.) And use that method all the time. It will not wear out. The next week, talk sports. After all, everybody watches European leagues, except you. So next Saturday, take two minutes talking teams and coaches and football superstars signing the million-euro contracts for terms they won't finish. Your tenor singers will be more than happy. Then start singing. They'll be charged. The following Saturday, begin the meeting with international politics. They must feel they have a rounded head. They'll be your friends. The naughty band will thin out. After all, that's what we want. *Morale: Do not keep hammering naughty attitudes in public.* It gives a show of insecurity. Rather, keep working on what they want to hear, what they want to sing, what they want to wear. And your choir goes on strong.

What about jokes? They work wonders. Make a joke on those naughty ones instead of a noise. Spot their inadequacies, and make fun of them in such a way that they themselves would laugh. In fact, it's so wonderful to be able to get a laugh out of a choir. You already learnt that choristers want a fun place to be in. Take a chance on that.

A word or two of caution. One, some people get worse than bad when anyone makes a joke about them, especially girls (not ladies). They just can't laugh it off. They take offence. They rot inside. Before you know it, you have a worse enemy than you began with. With them, you should be very careful. They might even want to get back. But if you have a humorous choir, you have a great place where bass singers can kid tenor singers while sopranos and altos laugh their heads off. Next Saturday is sure to be fun. Everyone is looking forward to it.

Two, a joke is not a joke when it is not *said* like a joke. You've heard it said that a joke is in the telling. You'll realise what I'm saying the day you run into some guy whose every word makes you laugh. Many of such guys hardly laugh themselves when they say the things. Some of them even wonder why people laugh too much too often at their words. It's in the way these people talk. If you can make a joke and no one catches it, you have not said anything. Keep your jokes to yourself then. But if it can make you really laugh, it probably will work on some others.

Your aim, summarily, is to make a friend out of a 'foe' so that you can have a great place to come to and great people to lead. Don't people make places?

*   *   *

One more thing. If you are a young man who has a pair of eyes and can see, you will agree that the choir is the sole department that brings the most beautiful and the prettiest girls together. We have slim ones, fat ones, tall ones, not-so-tall ones, fair ones, dark ones, and chocolate ones. We have white ones, black ones, red ones, and, sometimes, green ones. Be careful. I'm not saying the girls in the choir are bad. I'm not saying the choir is a dirty gathering of filthy feminine fools. But if you care about your future and like to learn from history rather than be a subject of repulsion on others' lips, you realise early that the choir is the easiest place to miss it.

If you are single, it's wise to allow yourself to simply fall in love as long as you're ready for love's responsibilities. The only caution is, never allow yourself into anything stupid, especially if you're a young lady. There just might be one or two guys aiming to take advantage of you.

If you are a man, your yoke might be easier apart from the fact that there might be one or two ladies aiming at you at the same time. Don't be surprised that both of them might know about each other's intentions or even hate each other as passionately as they each seem to desire you. (Ladies get talking, you know.) Having these two ladies (or more) to manage in the same choir might be a task. You are advised never to take advantage of anyone. These things have happened throughout history. No lady is foolish enough not to spot talent when she sees it. The smarter ones go for whom they believe has potential. Realise, then, that you are on the spot. Be prepared to love one and no more at a time, if you must love at all in this sense. It might just be your chance of finding a virtuous woman. There's hardly any easier way. You're working for it though. Learn all you can. Just don't think it's cool to play games. You may be rudely shocked what you'll find if you do.

Girls today are not really stupid like *you think* those of those days used to be. They'll do anything to hurt whoever dares to hurt them. So the wise man learns to treat them with even greater respect than he gets in return. That's the guy who wins the queen. This is your chance.

I hate to share the case of an unmarried pastor who had an affair with his assembly's single choir mistress with the promise of marriage. The young woman happened to be a close friend. So I went into our little town to schedule rehearsals over a season for a special rendition, combining choristers from three denominations. The lady had waited quite long for Mr Right, and being better financially, she became a target for this minister. To cut it short, she got pregnant, they got invitation cards out, and when donations didn't come in as expected, the guy called it all off. The cart already got before the horse, so the walls came a-tumbling down in a rollercoaster crash. The lady mysteriously miscarried, and we all had to live with the public disgrace we were dragged into for some guy who went completely wild.

Now, to the married ones. Persuade your spouse to cooperate with your sexual needs, or you are both headed for trouble should you have a real challenge of activity in that area of your life. It's not too strange to find that some lady in your choir doesn't care about the size and lustre of your wedding band. It's no longer news that some would so bluntly ask you out for 'a piece of the cake'. Crazy, you may think. Not in our denomination, you may say. But take a ride to your denomination's parish located in the city. Your mouth might drip some juice at what you'll find. Wisdom, then, is to come to terms with the particles suspended in our fast-flowing current and see that the whole world is really within the grasp of the evil one. And that you are supposed to be wiser than the children of this world in their own generation. Many times, you'll seem to belong to an earlier generation though. If you can't play their game by their terms, you'll be labelled old-fashioned. But you know you are the salt of the earth and cannot afford to have communion with darkness, whichever way it shows up. So you take a stand.

Tell your wife what is going on, especially if she's not in the same choir (and I advise that she should not be so your sense of judgment is not beclouded on the one hand and your sense of love and devotion is not misjudged on the other). Let your understanding of the unique situation guide you through whether to paraphrase or give details. Make sure that whatever you do is in the best interest of your marriage. Nothing should suggest to your spouse that your love might be at risk, that their beauty or handsomeness is being tested in keen competition. Keep your fire burning. Keep reassurances coming. Your love is all your spouse's got. No one can truly give you anything better, sweeter, purer, or lovelier than you are already getting. Therefore, turn off the lustful suitors. Make them see every time that there's nothing left of you for anyone else (for some might offer to just have a taste of you, whatever that means). These things in all their shades, shapes, colours, and sizes can be really tempting. You must be quite resolute in your decision to stand through it all.

There's nothing to fear though. You'll weather the storm. It won't last. It may come and go from time to time. Realise that it goes with the territory—any territory, for that matter, where men and women in their active years have to be together for some worthy cause. You only need to make a decision about how you'd react should your temptation show up where a higher human authority is not around. Be wary of errors. Let them irritate you. When you are predetermined, the whole thing is easier.

If someone asks you for something, you have the upper hand. In a sense, you are superior. You are the one who decides to give or not. The asking may be subtle. If you think something's up, something might really be up. Man is naturally telepathic. You are picking signals. From that moment on, make a firm decision never to fall. If you can avoid being alone with such and such a sister, see to it that that is exactly what you do! Whether you can or not, keep doing your work well, but keep your eyes open.

Should you fall and should get hurt, take His word and clean up your mess. This may not be easy. You must know that there is a throne of mercy to which you may come. There is healing for your soul. You saw that it was wrong, yet you did it and then realised how far beneath you have fallen. It may feel like the fall to a thousand feet below sea level. But there's hope for a better, more fulfilling life. Do not dwell where you are and do not go further down. There's still a use for you in the Potter's house. Let not anyone rejoice over you. You can get back up again. Please, don't die there. You only need an act of will—the strength that seems lacking. Please, come back home. Stand up straight. Wash your face and walk in grace. Walk back to your choir, and take that place of service, resolved never to repeat your mistakes.

There are some folks who want to make the same mistake all over again. Of course, they are like a dog which returns to its vomit. They feel they can always ask forgiveness every time. No matter how prone and predisposed you may think you are, beyond that one-time crucifixion, there is no remission for intentional revelling in filth like a pig in the wallow by compulsion. If sin has dominion over a soul, his situation is pathetic indeed. He needs help. Such a one should cry out, or he may be on the way to perdition. The arch enemy has no mercy at all and seems more ruthless with the strong and lofty than with the meek and lowly yet would destroy the former or the latter with the same swiftness and certain sadism with which history is so conspicuously replete. Be wise and seek to stay in your calling. This might be your test of faith. Stay strong and stand firm. In all thy doing, put thy body in check!

THE CHORALE

Basic Harmony

. . . .

Music has always been a part of humanity. In all cultures, it still exists in some form of folk music. And all folk music is based on some kind of system or order of notes. The earliest for which history can account are the Greek modes. Even those did not survive the fall of the Greek empire. The Byzantine modes that we all came to know trace their origins, if only by name, to those of Greece. It is from these modes that we got our present-day diatonic scales.

The diatonic scale consists of two forms—major scale and minor scale. Their notes may be described with respect to keys (A, B, C, D, E, F, G). (Musical notes are named after the first seven letters of the English alphabet.) Their notes may also be described by degrees (I, II, III, IV, V, VI, VII). Their notes may yet again be described by technical names (tonic, supertonic, mediant, subdominant, dominant, submediant, leading note). Finally, their notes may be described by sol-fa (*doh, ray, me, fah, soh, lah, te*). Often, the first note is repeated to make a scale of eight notes. Note that the order of the notes depend on the form of the diatonic scale being considered.

Should we run the major scale in the key of C, we have the following:

Keys	C	D	E	F	G	A	B	C'
Degrees	I	II	III	IV	V	VI	VII	VIII/I
Technical	*tonic*	*supertonic*	*mediant*	*subdomt.*	*dominant*	*submedt*	*leading*	*tonic*
Solfa	doh	ray	me	fah	soh	lah	te	doh

On the piano, these are white keys. But it helps to think of black and white keys as equals. That way, there is a key between C and D. There is also a key between D and E. But there is no key between E and F. So we say that the distance between C and D is a tone. But the distance between E and F is a half tone or a semitone. That is how the major scale is constructed; otherwise, we won't have the *doh, ray, me, fah,* . . . sounds progressing. Similarly, between B and C, there is no black key. So here again, we have a semitone. We, therefore, conclude that there occurs a semitone between the third and fourth notes of the major scale and between the seventh and eighth notes.

Now, you may begin the major scale from anywhere on the piano, but you must follow the pattern of construction described above. In which case, if you intend to run the major scale in G, you begin with G. You will end up with all white keys except the seventh note, which will be black. (Remember, there has to be a semitone between the seventh and eighth notes of the major scale.) So the seventh note in the key of G is raised from F (which is white) to F sharp, next to F on the right (which is black). We use the word *sharp* because we moved rightwards. A sharp (#) is an *accidental*. Another accidental is called a flat ("). Accidentals are signs used to alter the pitch of notes. A sharp raises the pitch of a note by one semitone, like F to F sharp. Whereas a flat lowers the pitch of a note by one semitone, like B to B flat.

So G major scale (the key of one sharp) would run like this:

Keys	G	A	B	C	D	E	F#	G'
Solfa	doh	ray	me	fah	soh	lah	te	doh

Similarly, D major scale (the key of two sharps) would run this way:

Keys	D	E	F#	G	A	B	C#	D'
Solfa	doh	ray	me	fah	soh	lah	te	doh

F major scale is the key of one flat.

Keys	F	G	A	B♭	C	D	E	F'
Solfa	doh	ray	me	fah	soh	lah	te	doh

There are two forms of the minor scale used today—harmonic and melodic. Let's consider the minor scale in A for easy illustration:

A harmonic minor scale:

Keys	A	B	C	D	E	F	G#	A'
Solfa	lah	te	doh	ray	me	fah	se	lah'

A melodic minor scale, ascending:

Keys	A	B	C	D	E	F#	G#	A'
Solfa	lah	te	doh	ray	me	fe	se	lah'

A melodic minor scale, descending:[1]

Keys	A'	G	F	E	D	C	B	A
Solfa	lah	soh	fah	me	ray	doh	te	lah

*   *   *

At this stage, you do not necessarily have to worry about the details of complex contrapuntal harmony. Be not denied if you wish. Gather texts on the subject. But if you'll allow your mind to settle, you'll find that all you should worry about is the voices you have to deal with right now and that all other advanced subjects may be reserved for composers, arrangers, and conductors of the orchestra. Again, there's nothing wrong with knowing so much.

To what should you give your attention? If you have not auditioned the choir (that's the first thing you should have done), begin right away. This means to group the voices that are alike factually and physically but respectively. The very next day of your choir practice, call each person, one after the other, to the piano. Then sound middle C and have the person reproduce that note with their voice. Then keep playing the next notes one by one till you reach the note beyond which the person being auditioned cannot go. Depending on the voice groups (or parts), your singers would fall into, broadly speaking, four categories—soprano, alto, tenor, and bass.

Soprano singers generally sing from middle C to the C an octave higher and then beyond to the G above that—give or take a few higher or lower notes.

---

[1]   Notice that the melodic minor descends in a different way from how it ascends.

Alto singers should sing from the G below middle C to the next G and then up to the next C (above that G).

Tenor singers would sing from the C one octave below middle C, then up to middle C and then the G after that.

Bass singers would sing from F below tenor C and up to middle C.

Remember that these are only guidelines. Expect to find folks who would get beyond, oftentimes below, your target notes for a part. Don't bother about that. Sometimes, I find somebody who would do fine in any two parts. Fix such people where they more naturally tend or where there is a higher need. *Morale: discretion.* You're the choirmaster, aren't you? The buck stops at your desk.

What we have just been through together is called *voice compass.* Now, broaden your horizon. Every individual has a compass—in the same sense as every musical instrument has a compass. The soprano recorder's compass is two octaves and a tone. But the concert grand piano has over seven octaves (eighty-eight keys in all). So you see the point. Be not perturbed if there are a few guys overshooting your own compass. What makes a leader stand out is knowledge as well as the maturity he can garner for effectiveness.

* * *

In any case, you should also know how the voices are combined for singing together. Each voice sings a note at a time. To sound two or more notes at a time, you'll need two or more voices, naturally. This way, we say you have a *chord*—two or more notes sounded together.

However, if you have a chord of two notes only, we speak in terms of the distance between these two notes. For instance, a soprano sings a C; then (or at the same time) an alto sings a G. We say you have an *interval.* An interval is the distance between two notes. So if your soprano sings a C, and your alto also sings the same C, you have a unison, meaning that there is no distance as such. They both sang the same note C. Whereas, if the soprano sings a D while the alto retains her C, the distance (interval) is a second. If you check this on the piano, the illustration is clearer.

Hence, if the soprano sings E while the alto retains C, we have a third interval. And so on. You may wish to read more about intervals.

A *triad* is formed when you have a chord of three notes, that is, you have two intervals, say C, E, and G. There is a third interval between C and E and another third interval between E and G. Because there are three notes now, we say we have a triad. The soprano now sings the uppermost note G, and the alto sings E while the tenor sings C.

All harmony is based on this simple principle of triads, depending on the key in which the singers sing their song.

Let's take an example. The choir sings a song in C major. If you build a triad on the first note of the C major scale, you'll have three notes, each a third interval apart: C, E, G. The first note on which the triad is built is *root*, that is C. Then E is called *third*. And G is called *fifth* because G is a fifth interval above (or ahead of) C. Whereas if you build a triad on the second degree (II) of the same C major scale, you'll have D as *root*, F as *third*, and A as *fifth*.

Basic harmonisation begins with primary triads which consist of the triads built on the first, fourth, and fifth degrees of any diatonic scale. This implies that if you are in the key of C, your primary triads are C, E, and G (with C as *root*); F, A, and C (with F as *root*); and G, B, and D (with G as *root*).

If you wish to experiment, choose three people from your choir—one representing each part (soprano, alto, and tenor). Let the soprano sing the fifth in each case, while the alto sings the third, and the tenor sings the root. You'll like what you'll hear, especially if you try it in the key of G. In this case, your primary triads become G, B, and D (with G as *root*); C, E, and G (with C as *root*); and D, F sharp, and A (with D as *root*).

To write harmony for your choir, though, you'll need to know more than this. You'll only need to take a study of harmony after you have understood the basics. But nothing stops you from taking your choir through harmony already written and available in several thousand scores within your reach. With only a couple of theory classes, you are doing wonders with the voices at your disposal. Please, do not hesitate to contact me if you wish to know which theory training satisfies your needs.

So far, we have considered primary triads of the major scale. They are all said to be *major triads* due to the intervals between the notes. These are only a type of triads. There are other types—minor triads, augmented triads, diminished triads. These are subjects of further study. Sometimes, even a major triad is made to sound different by the addition of a seventh, that is, the note higher than the fifth by a third interval. Scientifically, this is a discord, but nowadays, aural tolerance has adapted sevenths as convenient concords so much so that lovers of jazz and even gospel music have come to bask in the liberty taken by contemporary composers.

With time, you would want to consider a study of non-harmonic notes which make your music even more acceptable. If you are really a new choirmaster with no musical background, do not worry about them yet. Get the basics right to start with.

Beyond the Chorus

· · · · · · · · · · · · · · ·

Music. Music. Music. These are the three functions of a choir in church, school, or any community. Your responsibility as a choirmaster is to ensure that your choir delivers.

Many times, there are materials to work with. Sometimes, a leader wishes to flap his wings and fly. Before he reached the point where he wished to spread his wings and soar, he attempted to try those unfamiliar territories. Who am I to blame him? A choirmaster may, if he so desires, wish to write his very own song and, if he does his homework well, have the choir perform it. This is a self-rewarding experience.

If you are emotional, your tear glands may overflow the first time you hear your work performed. I recall one such experience. It wasn't my first time. The circumstances were just unique. I was rounding up in the university and didn't want to get burdened with choir practice, so I skipped that night. As I approached the academic arena from the hostel, I heard voices singing something familiar. I looked up the top-floor walkway (we ran rehearsals on walkways, you know), and yonder I saw lights! *My song! Oh, my song,* I thought. I was now fighting back the tears. I walked closer and stood right under the group on the ground floor, unknown to them, calming my goose pimples.

I wish to expend a few words to hint on the idea of writing your own songs or share the possibility of better songwriting. There are two ways to write a song: one, a tune rings in your head, and you add words to it; two, you have a text of words, and you set it to a 'singable' tune.

Experience says the latter works better than the former. If you are setting your words to a known tune, your work would be less original. If you do that, after a few years, you might hate the song altogether. It is more acceptable to use a common text than it is to use a common tune.

So let's explore our latter position. Whatever words you have ringing in your poetic mind or lifted from the pages of scripture, write it down on a piece of paper. If you are picking words from a book, say, someone else's poem, check copyright laws in your area.

Now, you have your words, maybe four lines, eight lines, many more lines, or even stanzas. I assume you have not studied theory of music enough to know what to do from here, so I will be less technical.

Begin with the first few lines. Read them aloud. This is where to add rhythm to the words using varying note value as each syllable reads. Then add pitch, at least one, to each syllable. You may add more than one note to each syllable. But there's no need to bother yourself too much. You'll learn to be thorough with time. All you need to know now is how to add pitch using solfa as easily as the rhythm naturally flows out.

Sing aloud many times to check 'singability'; familiarise with the tune and memorise the melody. If you have a tape recorder, record it and play it back to a friend or your sister. If they say it's fine, note how they say so. If it's said without reservation, believe it. If you don't have a tape recorder, use the sound recorder on your mobile phone. Be sure to register it immediately. Tunes seem to be winged creatures except you tie them down. It's better and easier if you can write music. Go straight to a desk, pull out a piece of manuscript sheet, and score it as is, say in C. Write a date and sign your name. File it away and continue later if you seem to run dry. Go back to it some other time to develop it. If you spend time with it, the song will grow. Before long, you may have a solo added to your little refrain. Maybe, tomorrow, you'll have a bridge.

Note that part of what makes a song a song is the element of *repetition*. Use it. Be sure to keep it simple, especially the refrain. Use repetition in the rhythm (how the notes flow out) and in varying pitch of lines. Let there be some similarities between the solo (or stanza) and the chorus (or refrain). Nothing needs to sound too strange from all the others.

Later, you may add a second, third, and fourth part. Again, record it somewhere. See that you give, by convention, the lead melody to soprano. Let alto finish somewhere around a fourth below the soprano. The tenor should almost always finish a third below the alto. Bass may finish even an octave below the tenor.

* * *

Choirmaster, now let's talk about *inversion*. A second (interval) consisting of C to D may be *inverted*. When this happens, the interval becomes a seventh, D to C. In the same way, triads may also be inverted so that the notes of the triad trade places. The 'original' triad consisting of, say, C, E, and G is said to be in *root position*. If you invert, so that C moves uppermost, you'd have E, G, and C. This is *first inversion*. If you invert again so that E moves uppermost next, you now have G, C, and E, *second inversion*.

An entire line of melody to be sung by your choir may be inverted in such a way that sopranos sing what tenors would have sung at a higher octave. Then, altos sing what sopranos would have sung. Similarly, tenors do what altos would rather have done. The effect is wondrous! It is something similar to a modulation in the ear of the layman. It's beauteous. I guarantee that some in your audience would think a modulation has occurred.

Well, then, what is a *modulation*? It is a change in key. A piece is written to begin in C and then changes to G. This is a dominant modulation because the G is dominant, relative to C. But when the modulation occurs, G becomes tonic in its own right so that we now have the tune performed as written in G major, say. Therefore, to modulate from C to G, the fourth note in C major is raised to F sharp. That is when the home key of G is felt as tonic.

The type of modulation described so far is 'natural' and is relative. There are other types of relative modulation. That in which the piece modulates from a major key to a minor key, or vice versa, is relative. To modulate to the relative minor, the fifth note of the old key is raised to become the seventh of the new minor key. Another one that is relative is that in which the piece modulates to the subdominant. In this case, the seventh note of the 'old key' is lowered (flattened) to become a fourth.

*   *   *

Another interesting thing you'll find as you lead your group is that your choir may not be able to perform a piece in the key in which it is originally written or recorded. The ideal thing is to insist that they do. With time, they'll get used to working by standards.

Sometimes, if only once in a while, you need to bend. I'll tell you why. Many soprano choristers in this part of the world are unable to do the said G. Many run a few notes short of that mark, though a good couple of notes above what your altos are doing. So you can't take them to alto for two obvious reasons: one, they sing many notes higher than alto singers; two, without a good number of soprano singers, your lead melody would be weak. Therefore, the best you can do, under the circumstances, is to let them remain in their part. But encourage them with drills to expand their current range, aiming at falsetto.

Here and now, though, you have a number to do, and they can't reach their highest note. Discretion allows you to drop the key of the song by a few semitones so the choir can practice or perform. Some of them may never even get beyond D—a ninth above middle C. So plan your change accordingly to suit the sopranos. Keep in mind that if you drop it too far, your bass singers will also complain of a low-pitch problem. So just a little drop would be sufficient. This change in performance pitch to suit performers is called *transposition*. It's simple. The tune is in E major, and you tell the organist to transpose to D—just a tone behind for convenience. After a few rehearsals, you may raise it a semitone. Then later, raise again. This trick is necessary if you are preparing for a combined choir performance, because at the mass choir rehearsal, no one would transpose for your choir. But you have to make your choir sing at home first.

Transposition may be necessary (if only initially) for a soloist, in which case, all definite pitch instruments playing with her may have to follow suit. As choir mistress, your duty is to try to discourage it.

There is one more transposition you can't do anything about. Certain musical instruments perform at a different pitch from the piano pitch so that if a piece is written for the piano in C, for example, they would need to play in another key to sound the same so that they might perform together. These instruments are called transposing instruments. An example is the B-flat trumpet. When it sounds its own C, what you hear is B flat on the piano. That is why it is called a B-flat trumpet. Since its sounding pitch is a tone behind the piano, the trumpeter has to perform a tone ahead to be able to play with the piano. The B-flat clarinet works the same way. Therefore, music for these instruments is transposed to the key in which they would play to sound the same as the piano (or other instruments). Oftentimes, the violin is tuned to the piano. So if music for the violin is in G, an accompanying B-flat clarinet would perform in A.

This takes us to the term *concert pitch,* which simply means *sounding pitch* or the pitch that is heard when an instrument plays whatever note(s) it plays. Half a century ago, the piano's A (at 440Hz, immediately above middle C) was agreed upon internationally to be concert pitch. It is to this pitch that all instruments tune while the orchestra warms up in readiness for a concert. Very many theory students have a challenge with that term. Help them out. You are choirmaster, aren't you? Like many terms in music, 'concert pitch' is stretched beyond this singular meaning. The pitch at which the piano plays in the midst of all other instruments is the one to which we refer to as concert pitch. This is clear if you remember that all of them tune to the piano's A. The clarinettist plays in B to be heard in A. So you see, our term is interesting.

But a choir mistress need not worry about too much academic and technical stuff. What is essential is the relativity between musical instruments should they have to perform together. The alto saxophone is an E-flat instrument, whereas the tenor saxophone is a B-flat instrument. This means the alto sax sounds a minor third ahead of the piano and should, therefore, play a minor third behind the key in which the piano plays in concert. It goes without saying that to sound A, the alto sax has to play F sharp while the tenor sax plays B.

Bubbles Burst

· · · · · · · · · · · · · · ·

Of every thousand student pianists, only one makes it to fame's platform. Yet even that fortunate one is not immune to the failure that can only be presented by a most trusted ally—his very own instrument. To appreciate this, you need to understand the background to which I like to refer to as the Pianist's Parkinson's, captured in the following four paragraphs.

He begins at the place others quit: rudiments. From then on to fingering and preparatory exercises up till his delight at his own first tunes, he pours through page after page of five lines and the spaces in between. The moment he begins mastering his favourite key of C, he has G to face and F to conquer or be vanquished by A flat. He runs at the scales to visit with masters before his age, such that from his first day before a synthesiser to his first night at the concert grand, he has seen several years of assiduous rehearsals daily, knowing that a day missed is made up for by another or two. With time, he reels out the notes of his first performance piece.

Oh the monster-saint of performance! Should he show up as a demon, the child pianist is cast out of the concert hall to seek some other career. Should he grace it as an angel of the spotlight with the blessings of Beethoven and Chopin, unto us is a child of wonder born, and the grease shall be upon his knuckles that the feet of all la belle monde beat a path to the repertoire of yet another prodigy of awesomeness at the eighty-eight keys. Performance is the place where he begins, the place where he peaks, the place where he flickers. Thus, he approaches each piece as though it were a performance, always seeking to make the appropriate impression, whether it be in the privacy of his home studio or in the grave quiet of a packed Carnegie hall. Whichever way it is: the pianist makes the performance, or the performance makes the pianist; no one can tell them apart, for nothing matters more than the ebonies and the ivories.

Be he self-trained, gone through a school of music, exercised under a tutor, or submitted to a mentor's challenge in a church choir, this one man has endured a soldier's regimen without a lash or a bullet wound. Yet there had been lashes of agoraphobia and the internal scars that curse the knuckles with pain, both from which he has been delivered. But never does he recover from the moment of hesitation before each first bar, the smoothness of a flawed scale flow, the sensitivity of replicated touch, or the rigours of precision dexterity featured only in privacy. These constitute the Pianist's Parkinson's—a caution to his soul or a quaking for his body.

So with hundreds of tunes played, volumes of hymns read, scores of maestro classical pieces fingered, and dozens of delicate jazz chords jammed, he arrives at a point where he seems to have seen it all. Nothing is sufficiently challenging any more than the perfectionism of a sniper. The great eagle begins to clip worn quills, pouring out his own masterpieces of improvisations for the next generations of pilgrims seeking conquests of mythical and mystical legends of the score.

But then, the same instrument that took him up the crest of his career bears the chance of a twist in fate that plunges him through the trough down below.

Everyone who has ever taken a training in aviation flight and safety procedures knows that the same bird that pierces through the clouds, climbing to 35,000 feet, can lose a third of that altitude in a split second almost without any prior warning to the pilot who has come to trust it with his very life. Clear-air turbulence, it is called.

Coastal locals know for a fact that the best swimmers sometimes find disappointment at the cost of dear life in the sport they love most when preying sharks or contorted currents choose to distort men's strengths into hapless weaknesses. Destiny, you may say.

The pianist should have learnt what a pilot always knows passes through a swimmer's mind and always gnaws at the souls of skylarks and tugs at the spirit of seamen. You are just about to smash your face into lines that may be put simply and summarily thus: *terrible things go with the territory*.

If you doubt it, ask a soldier. Visit a general in Africa's greatest fighting force in defence of the labour of our heroes past. Take a trip to any territory in international waters, the command of a four-star general in any wing of the world's strongest military power stationed in posts across the globe, and say if the Star-Spangled Banner does yet wave. Whether you think or think not that the bravest on the planet reviews *Rule Britannia* or the rules of engagement before he sets sail with troops high enough in morale to take on a host of angels, you will return to me with the mantra of the worthiest religion: *content to fill a soldier's grave*. Why? Because the world's finest military officers know there is a chance of failure at the cost of human lives.

So cheer up, sister. When it comes to a choir performing, at least human lives are not at stake. The error of a doctor would almost certainly cost a life. If it's the case of an engineer, his first mistake may be his last. Therefore, take heart, and take it easy.

Sometimes, the choir fails. One part messes up and wrecks the performance. The vocalist damages the lead. Instrumentalists play complete nonsense. Or even you get on the conductor's platform without a piece and completely forget the arrangement; thus, an entire rendition is ruined. What else can go wrong? It's a convention with international guests on a night when sound department does its work so well that every piece of rubbish your choir sings is heard; an invitation to an event with other excellent choirs present; a competition for which you have rehearsed through a lot of pain and creativity; or your patron's seventieth birthday with senators, governors, diplomats, professionals, and business moguls in attendance. Then your choir fumbles.

Let me show you my wounds. When I began choir training programmes across denominations, the first contract I signed went well until one day. The choir messed up so badly, I was so shocked when the congregation began to applaud so loudly and for so long. When I told my mother, she laughed so uncontrollably, you couldn't imagine how confused I all the more became.

In December 2000, I was a young enthusiast trying to do great things. I planned a town-wide concert and pulled choristers from various denominations under the umbrella of Badagry Mass Choir. We scheduled rehearsals over a six-month period, invited musicians from out of town, plus a couple other excellent choirs from the city. We scheduled age-old numbers and tough contemporary numbers that have won platinum at the Grammy's. We worked hard at it all. Some of them were numbers we were all to do together in one voice—about a hundred voices. I worked with a team of decorators from about eight o'clock in the morning and descended from the ladder just before ten at night when the events were about to begin. The guests had begun to arrive. Video camera men set up their equipments while soundcheck went on simultaneously. Great ministers stepped in, and men I looked up to came in for the programme.

Now, what do you think my choir should do with every number we were scheduled to perform? Wondrous delivery. Right? That's exactly what they did with *almost all* the numbers we rendered. But with one in particular, they goofed. And so badly at that, there was no patching up.

Was that the time to bury your head in shame? No! Never! That is the time to focus on the good part of the night. That's exactly what a matured choirmaster does. But you and I, what do we do? We cast our head down low, give the group a *Thriller* look, and walk out on them while they are still on stage, compounding the confusion. If they like, they can sleep there for all you care. That would be worse than the performance you wish had gone better. If there's anything I've learnt all these years, it is this: Whenever my choir is at its worst with a rendition, *I never let them hear it from me.*

Tell yourself the truth. Do they know when they have done well? Do you think they don't know when they have fumbled? The answer is yes in each case. If you are a good and understanding choirmaster, they *don't need* to hear it from you. If you are firm and disciplined, they *hate* to hear it from you. If you are harsh and disrespectful, they *dread* to hear it from you. So think a little. What kind of work life would you rather have? What you don't need, what you hate, or what you dread? On the balance of probabilities, my guess is, 'none applies'. Why on earth would you give what you'd rather not receive? These people are humans. They have flesh and blood. They have feelings too. Treat them just the way you'd have others, especially superiors, treat you. *Morale: Do unto others as you would be done by!* Fair enough.

Since you know what not to do, let's discuss what to do in crazy situations like your choir messing up a performance. You focus on what they did right during the terrible performance or sometime in the past and comment on that. Let me give you an idea. I scribble a note and have them pass it around. My note usually reads something like this:

You are wonderful people. (I didn't say always.)

I'm proud of you no matter what. (Not only when you do it right.)

Nothing ever sounded better than the chorus. (They probably messed up the bridge.)

That next key was just too high. If only we didn't modulate. (So the rubbished modulation doesn't look like their fault.)

Thanks for doing your best. (Of course, their best wasn't good enough.)

In the north-western Nigerian state of Sokoto, I directed a 120-voice choir twelve years ago. There, I learnt there's something better to do than avoiding confronting them with woes after they burst your bubble. We had a song that required the best that each of us could muster, from conductor to lead vocalist to choristers to instrumentalists. My vocalist, Phatee, had done more than her best both in private and public rehearsals. I had delegated the music to an exceptional keyboardist, JB, who drove the bassist and drummer pretty hard as well as checked the sound himself. I drilled the rest of the voices over and over again. To my amazement, they found the work really arduous. These two people and another lady, Bertha, were the ones who invited me to work with this choir. The team which originally had the daunting task lacked the requisite skill to prepare these choristers pulled from various denominations for the biannual convention of a ministry that didn't have a church. Most of the singers came in for all-night rehearsals from higher-institution campuses. So they weren't so bad. But somewhere along the line, I saw that we were headed for trouble. I simply told Phatee we wouldn't do the song. Oh, how she pleaded! But I was sure that if we had done it, it would have amounted to an Olympic disgrace.

You must learn to see the errors before they occur so you may avoid them rather than avoid facing your people with it. JB took it in good stride. He could easily understand what I was doing and was not going to do. Of course, we did several other numbers together. We had fine beauteous moments, and everybody was happy. No one really wants 120 people messing up all at once.

THE CODA

Instructing Instrumentalists

• • • • • • • • • • • • • •

If you love concerts, I have an invitation for you. I know a place where they have a 1,000-man orchestra—the largest in Africa. Whoever becomes choirmaster there *plays at least seven instruments* to written music! Now, what that means is that their choirmaster, who probably directs the orchestra, plays violin, flute, clarinet, horn, trumpet, trombone, and the organ or a similar combination of seven different orchestral instruments and reads from printed sheet music to do so.

My friend, do you still *feel* like a choirmaster? And do you still want to come to the concert? What if an elderly man walks up to you asking you to give the closing remarks? That's exactly what happened to me the last time I was there. Of course, I gave a rousing speech.

These people happen to know that *knowledge* of *theory* and *practice* is critical to the leadership of a group that would excel musically. So naturally, they raised the bar. You can't walk tall among musicians if you don't even have an idea how they do what they do and why. Do you know what happens when a new conductor gets in front of an orchestra? I'll tell you. A test! Expect your first test from the trumpeters. You have had all the interviews before you got here? That's trash. The real test hits you when a trumpeter intentionally plays a phrase wrongly. They are not bad people. They are just trying to see if you practically qualify to lead them. My dear, it's not enough to earn a degree and think you are ready to direct a choir. You can have more degrees than a thermometer. You'll only get mad boiling over. You only lead if you know more.

You will find that the most difficult people to deal with in your choir are the instrumentalists. The whole thing only begins to make sense to you when you know what they know or more. You are a lot more in control if you are the very one who trained them. Now you see why it is good you play the instruments too. They may not even take you seriously when you invite them to a special rehearsal for vocalists and instrumentalists, except you are going to man an instrument or two. *Morale: To your theoretical knowledge, get ready to add skill.*

Recently, I was marrying music to voices in a choir practice when I found I could no longer stand the rubbish coming from the keyboardist. I had given him beginner lessons a few years earlier. Over the years, though, he had mixed with some of those boys whose keyboard music is all about sevenths. We were doing a solo piece with a mass choir backing up carefully arranged staccatos. The music for this piece consisted of a simple progression of primary and secondary triads. This young man kept adding a seventh to every chord. I didn't know when I burst out.

'Everything is not a seventh! It's not jazz!' And on I went in disgust.

You know how nauseating it is when you show someone a simple progression before choristers show up, and the next thing you hear is all sevenths. Gosh!

Apart from fundamental knowledge, you yourself must *be very familiar with the piece* you're working on. Know it like you know your five fingers. Become an authority on this particular song. That's why it's important to gather your lieutenants first. Begin with the instrumentalists. Then set up an appointment with your vocalists. Arrange a third meeting, if you have to, for both instrumentalists and vocalists, before you take the song to the general choir. That way, you would have pruned off all the rough edges, and the whole thing works excellently.

You cannot get familiar with the piece if you do not understand *the peculiarity of its style*. I just hinted to you that sevenths are very much acceptable in jazz. That does not mean that there are no sevenths in other genres.

Broadly speaking, all chords may be divided into *concords* (or consonance) and *discords* (or dissonance). Aside from the scientific details, concords are those chords that are aurally accepted as pleasant; their constituent notes are in harmony. Discords, however, give a harsh, 'jarring' feeling to the ear. Major triads are concords, and sevenths fall into the category of discords. Over the centuries, though, with composers experimenting and improving their art, a couple of discords became *aurally tolerable*. Sevenths are one of such chords.

But when the first chord is a seventh, and the next is a seventh, and then the very next chord is also a seventh up to the first cadence, the piece might just have been 'jazzified'. So check the other elements of jazz music. And if you find them there, you probably have a jazz piece on your hands. If you know this, your study of the piece becomes easier because you are familiar with the peculiarity of the style.

This advice might just come in handy. It is the rule that guides the treatment of a discord: *preparation* and *resolution*. Get your instrumentalists (if they play without a score) to prepare the listener before a discord is played, then to resolve the discord to a concord after the discord is played. Your music will sound better.

Similarly, a choirmaster should also be familiar with *the peculiarity of his instrumentalists*. Everyone is unique. Get used to broad strokes and get used to specifics. Read carefully the chapter on the naughty-natured, and you might not have a lot to worry about in this chapter.

There's this choir I had trained in some time past. They recently had a concert and invited me about two weeks before the event to assist in some way. On the evening of the concert, I was in a pastor's office when one of the ministers raced in to alert me of the musical chaos going on in the auditorium. You see, I had delegated much of the administrative assignments. Most of what was left had been arranged before I was invited anyway. The 'chaos' this minister now worried about was caused by the latter. I'll explain. They asked some weird boys to come in and play some weird instruments. When the weird boys got in, they chose to play their weird instruments in weird ways. I simply got in, assessed the situation in seconds, threw the boys out into the congregation, and made a few changes among my own instrumentalists. In that instant, the entire praise music changed. Everything made sense.

You see, I didn't have to be there when the programme opened. Besides, no one told me they had invited some people to play something terrible in very terrible ways. You must be able to work similar magic. But learn from my errors; I should have double checked to make sure I knew everything that had been organised to happen. Be in control if you can't be everywhere to save the day.

I have seen instrumentalists get in a programme to constitute themselves a disgrace to the music profession, exhibiting a debasement of artisanship as their idea of maestro substance. I recall an assembly that hired a flutist who didn't play a note Sunday in and Sunday out but carried a follower to the choir stand with the name of the music school he came from. That became his emblem. He and his boy always wore dirty jeans, sleeveless shirts, and pairs of very flat sandal slippers that dragged after them, and they had bushy, unkempt hair. There was another assembly where they had hired a talking drummer who had an untidy little boy trailing behind him all over the platform with an aura of disregard for everything sacred, prim, and proper.

I've seen many roughly managed concerts where instrumentalists who never attended any rehearsals gathered very roughly indeed around the instrument corner on the stage, doing practically nothing. Oh yes, they do something. When a drummer gets up from his stool, they quickly take his place to try their raw talent at a major event, with neither rehearsal nor training. What a shame!

Equally important is the fact that your *vision* must be clearly understood by your musicians. If it takes you four weeks to share it with the choir in bits per time, be sure that it takes you a quarter of that time or less to share it with your musicians. Choose how you do this very carefully. They must not feel you are trying to use them to achieve your own egotistic objectives, if you are not. Communicate your ideas with a good measure of respect for their feelings. Remember, these are your lieutenants. Some respect must go with the command.

One more thing. Palestrina was choirmaster at St John Lateran in the sixteenth century. Did you know that he resigned because the choirboys were poorly fed? Now that you are choirmaster, take a cue from that Italian organist and composer by seeing to it that your musicians are taken care of. If they are on the payroll, be sure no delay occurs. When I engage extra hands for concerts, I don't only pay for the event, I ensure my instrumentalists are paid for rehearsals also.

Managing Ministers

• • • • • • • • • • • • • •

You don't want to read this chapter because you are minister of state in charge of your school choir. Well, you need to. The minister above you is the school principal. You don't want to read this chapter because you engineer a community choir. Well, then, the pilot in command—the lord mayor—is your minister. And if you lead a church choir in addition to your school choir and village choir, you must learn to manage your bosses. I'll be frank. This is the bitter part of a sweet pill.

Four years ago, I had the privileged responsibility of working a choir that I would have considered good enough without my help. The implication is self-evident: you had better produce results *now*, or you are *absolutely irrelevant*! Naturally, I chose the former. Let's call it Victory Temple Choir. I was lucky to connect with VTC a couple of days before the contract was signed. Pretty good head start! By the time I got in full view of the congregation, days after the official proposal introduction, I launched a short, powerful rendition that sprang the reverend to his feet to share the word. I'll never forget how he repeatedly proclaimed, 'That is what a training can do!' But we had just begun.

You don't need to be told. There's a two-pronged principle everyone who works a choir on contract bears in mind: *one, tick says the clock, tick, tick! Two, he who pays the piper calls the tune!*

The boss expects results *now* because you are on the payroll! Wisdom demands that you pick simpler songs first, projecting yourself two weeks in advance. Begin immediately, and work as though your very life depends on it. Do not assume that choristers would feel your pulse on cue. They won't! Share all the signals you wish they get, and concentrate all your energy on the songs. Realise that the minister who gave you a job *today* 'expects' results *yesterday*! Believe me, he does want magic. Why? Because he's paying, dear. *Morale: Tick says the clock.*

Quite importantly, know also that he wants what he likes! So take your attention away from the music that moves you. Find out exactly what ministers to him, and work earnestly at it. You are likely to last longer. When you get tired of the place, get foolish. How do you get foolish? Just minister the songs the minister dislikes. Security will escort you out the gates. *Morale: He who pays the piper calls the tune.*

Music history has it that musicians a thousand years ago were commissioned by patrons. These patrons were priests, reverends, pastors, kings, queens, and noblemen. Thus the musicians of those days led pauperised lives whenever they displayed a lack of understanding for this eternal maxim. Smart musicians rather learnt to compose, rehearse, and perform tunes that the lord who paid the piper favoured, to the exclusion of all else. Remember that Handel composed *Water Music* just because King George I commissioned him to. The music was performed simply for the king and his guests on barges over the River Thames several times that night on the command of His Royal Majesty. How dare you choose to perform anything that makes sense only to you! Darling, you don't have to like it. If the boss finds it wonderful, it indeed is wonderful enough. Never forget the Chinese proverb, *'If you have money in your pocket, you are wise, you are handsome, and you sing well too.'*

Let me illustrate with a personal experience. When I began working with VTC, what I did well was a beauteous first impression. My challenge was somewhere else however. I like to have a choir play each piece of music to type, sounding like it would if it were performed anywhere else. Standard, it is called. The choir, therefore, rehearses the four parts of the hymns for each week. The pianist or organist must play according to the score. Nothing improvised if it's not an interlude. Save the improvisations for jazz. The same goes for any genre for that matter. But in this church, after a few weeks of perpetrating 'my blunder', the reverend called me into his office for a sermonette on 'upbeat' hymns. So he called it. I learnt my lesson, pretty late though. *Morale: When you are in Rome, do as a Roman.*

I sound too blunt, I know. But I'm not just making things up. I have worked with ministers all my youthful life, and it's no burden to feel their pulse. Nevertheless, in writing this chapter, I scheduled an interview with a minister I respect to ensure that I'm not just leading people to see only through my eyes.

The pastor shared with me the reality of today's church system from the stark contrast between our two extremes in five crystal clear 'm' words. You may wish to think of it as my paraphrase: By reason of the complexity of today's life, he said, a good majority of *ministers* are caught within the web of seeking a good number of *members,* which translates into a good amount of *money* achievable by a good dose of *music* serving as catalyst for a good ration of *message.* Never forget that! In fact, reread that sentence before you go to choir practice every week so you might get a cute idea about how crucial your assignment is.

By reason of the complexity of today's life, a good majority of ministers are caught within the web of seeking a good number of members, which translates into a good amount of money achievable by a good dose of music serving as catalyst for a good ration of message.

Cut out that sentence, run copies, and paste one of them on the dashboard of your car so you won't miss it as you drive to church. Stick another copy to the front cover of your hymnal so you will see it every time you prepare for the next hymn. Tape yet another copy to the centre of your piano music stand where you will see it before you play each piece. Wrap one more copy of that sentence around your baton so you can glance at it before you stand the choir up to perform a special rendition. Keep one copy in your face powder pouch so you might paste it on after your performance bathes your face with sweat and oil. It's not a sentence you want to forget. For your sake!

You don't have to agree with me. As I write this chapter, bottled within me is a tall measure of caution. However, with the canonisation of the magniloquent doctrine of mass, massive and multiple offerings, with denominations springing franchises per second laden with a non-negotiable responsibility of financial flourishing and pressured remittance, with the establishment of ivy-league schools priced out of reach of average citizens by the same church authorities that coerced them into 'giving', and with the rising toll of black priests in training cast out after many years of *Trading Places* experiences, one cannot be sure what focus the church now has or what force now seems to drive her so vigorously towards it. The church house runs on the grease of money in the code word *offering* just like the state house runs on the wheels of money in the code word *tax*! What remains is for you and I to do the best we can of the business committed to our care.

Succeeding by Succession

• • • • • • • • • • • • •

Let me continue the story I promised I'd share with you about the congregation choir of an Assemblage of God church I had to run for four days. The group had been arranged to split in two to continue the work. So that necessitated two leaders—musically speaking. They had leader figures already. But that wasn't sufficient for the purpose of function. By the second day, I launched the work I had to do. I had done a rearrangement of their request, contemporised it a little for SATB. We ran on it, and the tonic solfa was fine. We began playing with the tune using other vowels and consonants. This would let the parts sink in. By this time, our schedule was about done. When the third night came, some people who had not been there the first two nights showed up. I kept scheduling auditions. There were also some who came the first night but didn't manage to show up afterwards. Well, we went on with the lyrics. It began to synchronise with the tune.

The previous night, I had nominated part leaders. So this night, it was time for conductors of the two groups to emerge. Someone in the group had studied music with a National Certificate in Education to prove it. He naturally qualified as one. There was this other person who had both experience and passion. In a sense, they were at the same level. The reason is that I had introduced a special sign language for live conduction which I learnt from my friend in New York through a French professor of music. This would help to direct dynamics in performance quite easily. They had to learn that, and they tried.

I had one day to go. It was the night of the experiment that I could view. So I put the conductors on the stand and sat at the electronic keyboard to accompany and to watch what my 'babies' would do, having been born twenty-four hours before. That night passed, and the day of the performance came. I sat as one of the judges and had a good time. Each group looked massive, and the singing was really good for four nights of preparation. Then, I sat to a sumptuous lunch at the parsonage. What d'ya expect? Good, good, good time.

This good time happened because I took the initiative to plant people who would succeed me after I had left. Everyone has to leave at some point, in life or in death. Maybe you'd be able to look back after you're gone to see what's going on. If or when you do, would you be sad, or would you be glad? The only way to earn the latter is to look into the house and put it in order. Plan and execute it as though you might be leaving tomorrow. The people would still need a leader when you are no longer there. And you'll not always be there. So get your hands on deck, in search of a replacement for yourself.

I led one such choir for two years, musically speaking, before I was offered its leadership, administratively speaking. You remember the choir I told you about, whose leader was not musically sound. When I began, I worked tirelessly, needless to say, for eight more years, until I thought it was time to leave. During my eight years, I had nominated an assistant and secretary to church leadership. The nominations were approved. The people served beside me. We had a great time together. With these people, I didn't need to worry about certain things. I will not forget their services. My assistant stood in whenever I travelled. She helped with relations with choirs of other churches. She helped with translations of my songs into local languages. She led praises many times. She did great.

My secretary worked the choir musically, while the assistant worried about choir administration in my absence. He prepared our letters and several transcriptions, especially those long Handel's that I enjoyed so much. While my assistant was alto part leader, my secretary was tenor part leader. You see, I had two parts less to worry about most of the time, apart from oversight functions. My secretary responded more than anyone else to my music classes. No wonder he served as pianist when I had to concentrate more on voices. He did quite well with bookkeeping.

Now, don't you wonder what I had to do as choirmaster? That's the benefit of the delegation I've been talking about. Of course, I decided what songs we did. I transcribed much early on before I could train someone to do it. (In those days, there was not much sheet music transcribed into tonic solfa for voices around here.) I proofread every transcription before copies were made. I ran the rehearsals and planned special programmes in great detail. I featured the choir in church every week. I gave classes periodically to groom the house. I ran vocalists' rehearsals and physical exercises. I related between the choir and church authority. I wrote songs for the choir to do and arranged music for it. I took out the choir on invitation. I drew an annual budget and function plan to the authority. I wrote a constitution because I didn't meet one. I upheld the highest disciplinary standard known in that assembly till now. I hired extra musicians for special programmes and saw to it that they were paid as and when due.

Yes, I did all that, but what is quite important, I tell you, is that I resigned leaving leadership options in the hands of church authority between my assistant and secretary. I'm glad they chose well and not outside these two.

Sometimes, it is difficult to leave. But I had to leave, and leave I did. There may be many reasons why people leave a place of service, but the reason for which someone leaves might be well known to him. I left because I saw it was time to leave. I had served enough after eight years. Someone else should be in the lead. Besides, I could see the possibility of a leader for the assembly, with whom I was sure I could not serve. If you learn anything, learn to choose with whom you serve. It counts for destiny. I had to take a bow and leave the stage when it became necessary to do so. When it becomes necessary for you to do so, I pray you'd know. Because you may not have sufficient time to prepare, I suggest you begin planning your exit now. Choose someone to whom you may pass on the torch. There's no greater task ahead of you. Remember that nations are ruined for this one reason of erroneous succession. Others are made eternally for the same reason of wise leadership transition. Remember the Man who handed His friends over to an equally able Comforter. He did so because succession is crucial to everything. May you find wisdom in the days ahead to be a great choirmaster who inspires a generation of talents and hands over to none less than the most suitable successor.

Outro

• • • • • • • • • • • • • •

The idea of a fitting agenda for choir practice surely occurred to me as I write this book, but the uniqueness of each choir's situation would not allow anything that may be referred to as quite general and ideal. Yours may be a church choir. Another man may have a school choir in his hands. Yet the woman on the other side of the Atlantic may be working with a community choir. There is yet a young lad working with a children's choir. And still you may just be the leader of a group of seniors planning a surprise rendition for those little babies who think they know so much. I do not believe that all these groups should use the same rehearsal plan when they meet. Besides, there are books in which there is an inclusion of choir-practice agenda. There is one more reason I didn't think it was necessary to include one here. One denomination may find it comely while another cannot find it applicable. What I sought to do is discuss the issues that may generally apply to most settings. If a choir practice plan is one of the reasons you bought this book, please forgive me, and let me know in writing, explaining your unique scenario, and I would be honoured to offer advice.

Nevertheless, there is a principle you should keep in mind as you plan each rehearsal. As a matter of fact, most of the challenges you face in rehearsal may never show up if you apply the strategy of the twenty-first century teacher in lesson delivery. First, sorry I never told you: you are a teacher too, a vocal music one. Second, the three-window principle about which I write has been used long before the twenty-first century by superior teachers.

'SOJ, just shoot!'

'All right, I will.'

Never appear before your choir with an all-talk-all-sing agenda! You must do better than that to engage everyone. If your choir is to perform for Easter, find an opera. Oh! What do they call that these days? A musical? Yeah, right! The former is performed live onstage; the latter is recorded and screened in the form of a film. Whatever you do, if your choir gets to act, if only once in a while, what they have to sing assumes a new meaning to them. Of course, you have less to worry about the ones who can't sit still for a while. If your audience can afford a dance, or some form of minimal movement, you are in luck. It's dancing time, dear.

Oh! Sorry, you don't dance. Can you stand my advice? Drag yourself to a dance school. After a few lessons, you'd find what's good for your group. Please, let them move. Some of them are dying right now. Save a soul, brother.

Before you get faster at springing standard stigma for the chorister who *can* learn in a way you *can't* teach, may I hop to the next? I will! The talk you do to them is fine. The movement is good. But very many of the folks you have there need to see something other than you in front. I know you. You have a vision of heaven and the heavenly. But trust me, choristers don't care. They'd rather see it too. So, dear friend, find a picture of heaven for your heaven song; you'll be glad, for they'll respond better. Project the lyrics of the song on the screen and be sure to put a very colourful picture in the background. Why? Some of your folks only hear by seeing, especially if there are any women there.

Speaking of women, these beautiful bundles possess very pretty visual strengths. Haven't you noticed that baby girls have larger eyes than their counterparts? Don't you know there are more blind men in the world than there are blind women? Do you not realise that of all the sighted persons on the planet, members of the fairer gender tend to possess better fashion senses and more precious ornamental tastes? How many times has your wife dragged you back from the door to get your doodle-toddler brain *redressed*? Do not pretend not to be guilty. We all are. Isn't it time you gave credit to these nonpareil pearls who pay the price of humble followership to sit in your choir and hear you yell down from your imperial heights, rattling about issues you don't even understand? Sincerely, you don't want to know about the sacrifices and the multiple tear-provoking bitter pills of duelling denials and complex constraints that three-quarters of your choir goes through. You may never be able to tell what love was greeted goodbye, what dislike was embraced with a smile, what pain and sickness are muffled under those bulky choir robes. Each time they smile at you, you have no idea what goes on in the lateral-thinking brain lobes which process the details that your tiny spectacled beads almost always miss. Therefore, if the only way you say thank you is by bringing them a relevant pictorial illustration of the piece to be performed, it is almost certainly worth it. Let the courage commanded by their graceful gait in procession and the vigour exuded by their pomp and pageantry in performance be worth stance and standard so priceless and rich that full showers of praise are summoned from depths within your committed heart. They are not your sword bearers. They are your soldiers. They marry the very essence of their motherly nature to the purest process of vocal production.

Dear Choirmaster, when they get pregnant, please send flowers if you can't visit with initial permission from the lucky guy. If they are single, learn now that it's not your place to judge. Even if you'd rather have her in the choir right now, don't show that silly part of you. Instead, take a tiny little gift with you. Something that says you love the baby she is carrying. The nausea and depression may be washed away if you are accompanied by a few singers to sing her a hymn. The healing power of music might just reach out and touch her.

Yes, it did touch my wife a couple of years ago when dislike for meals filled her fuller than the baby she was carrying. My favourite breakfast—omelette when it goes with a toast over the rich aroma of brewing coffee, plus the coffee itself to flush it down—became her nightmare. A man could tell you how uncomfortable life gets when he has to choose between his beautiful, loving wife and his steaming mug of Maxwell House, for the former is good to the last breath while the latter is good to the last drop. I didn't have to. My mother was called in, given her four-time personal experience in 'O and G'. It didn't work!

One night, I played a hymn tune and got compelled to do it every night afterwards. My *Lazarine* rose from the bed and made her way to the study! Now, what do you think would be our visiting 'doctor's' prescription?

'Son, you oughta play something every night!' It was more like an order. So I got an extra job at no extra pay.

But it's not only in my home that music does this deed. This healing power is evident in many religious meetings. There may not be a greater historical proof of supernatural influence on earth via the instrumentality of music in an attempt to alter the course of man's dealings with his other men than such words 2,500 years ago as 'But now bring me a minstrel . . .'

But how a soft, slow, and simple tune is able to work its way through the physiology of a distraught body and the psychology of a sickened soul may not find full expression in the eyes of a worried choirmaster though its continual reoccurrence remains a phenomenal fact. Whether musicologists know for certain what quality of tone, tempo, timbre, or texture exclusively holds the secret is a subject of evolving academic debate. What is undoubtedly accurate, however, is that, like the letters of all therapeutic oracles transmuted into the spirit of practice, its science seems concealed within its art so convolutedly that only the composer, producer, or arranger really knows the endgame that underscores a curative piece of printed music or a sequenced synthesis of a treatment soundtrack. Perhaps the trick is in the appropriate expression of a skilled performer before a live audience that springs the magic which defies definition.

Even if it is a combination of one and any other, what we know is that hospitals and clinics are swinging their doors open to pianists, violinists, and flutists in many parts of the world as study after study testify to the eternal truism of musical therapy. Therefore, before you contest the psalmist's story as he played on his harp in front of an ailing king, realise that therapeutic response in premature babies to such music as can heal is now confirmed science. My guitarist friend wrote his mother a song when she got down with a stroke. She began to recover.

Well, don't rule out the commerce. Healing music has begun wearing shelf life and flooding the pharmaceutical market, online and in stores. And they are properly packaged. Natural sound effects of birds chirping, oceans crashing, or whispering coniferous branches constitute the opening bars of a couple of them. Others catch your eyes with colourful scenery and superior graphics on the album jacket. Yet there are those done right with flamboyant sales pitches as in the scale of the music upon which the composition is based.

Whatever constitutes the packaging, its content remains our subject matter. Churning that potion of matter out in humility as it courses through the soul of the aged is crucial to everything. If anything, we must realise that disease may be the logical advance signal to the close of life. If we must age, we might as well brace ourselves.

Young though I am, I have enjoyed the company of the elderly for years. I have many times been struck in awe of their winning wisdom and wondered in a whirl at their waning woes. Does the loss of hair and health amaze you as much as the loss of semitones which deepen the pitch of their wondrous voices without warning? I really don't know which should. But amazing indeed is the situation where a few of these folks seek to give a performance in the midst of such chaos and trauma of a translation in a blur. Should this group of seniors seek to remain in the choir, treat them with the utmost respect. On them, the littlest exertion of energy from you is guaranteed. Should they attempt a group performance amongst their peers, see to it that they have all the help they need.

For instance, transpose the music down a tone when you accompany them. Mention it if they sing a note off its pitch. These people sincerely want a perfect rendition. They'll appreciate your comment. Let them choose their style though. You probably weren't even born then . . . Applaud them sincerely and never exaggerate, never flatter. Do not assume you are smarter. I can bet you are not. Remember, I spend a lot of time with them. Get the pieces for all other instruments ready, and encourage younger accompanists to be punctual. Very many of today's children seem pretty lax with rules and ideals.

If your choir of seniors doesn't want the robe, don't lure them. If they don't want your introduction, don't patronise them. Ensure, for the life of you, that the music is a super performance. They'll thank you for it.

Once, when I had a choir of men's fellowship, I wrote them the best song I ever have written; I prepared a soundtrack so that nothing could go wrong, depending on accompanists who don't care about the elderly on the one hand, and I could give them the pleasure of digitally programmed accompaniment. I also performed with them. The house exploded!

They are blunt. I love them for this one reason. They just don't care what you look like. They let you know if you are good. They have nothing to lose. They've been about the block a couple of times. They see the patterns in life quite more easily. In a nutshell, these guys have seen it all. Take their advice as seriously as you receive the low-price high-value gifts they sometimes toss in your chest.

Nine years ago, it was the wedding of a good friend of mine from school days. I had to make the trip with my own new bride. As a rule, I hardly socialised in those days. (Marriage has changed me.) To make me want to go, I arranged to have a function at the event. Naturally, my assignment fell around the choir.

As we checked into the hotel, I hurried to the rehearsal previously scheduled because the choir's special number was *Hallelujah* chorus. I got in to find it had been changed to *And the Glory of the Lord,* also from Handel's Messiah. Even so, the special rendition, as well as the hymns, was so good that as the wedding service ended, an elderly man managed, through failing footsteps, to advance towards me. He hadn't reached me when a smile of radiant joy lit his lean, wrinkled face, and he extended his hand. I quickly made for his hand with mine in hope for a good-morning presidential handshake. I was wrong. The hand had a bill folded in it. It was too late to turn it down. Choristers were just beginning to disperse because I had just concluded my thank-you address. I don't remember if there were tears in his eyes, but I was that much moved to tears myself. I took the old note he squeezed in my hand with a grateful heart, bowed to thank him, and stood glued to the floor for what seemed like a long time, thinking through his words, 'Well done. Thank you,' as he shook my hand and turned away. I haven't since recovered from that kind of appreciation. He couldn't even wait one moment longer, and I can't quite figure exactly what he looked like apart from his frame and the look in his eyes. That's how blunt these folks are. Celebrate them all the same.

When their children bring forth children, let much more joy fill your heart. Why? Another generation of choristers is being born. More tedious work for you. Well, it's not so difficult, but don't be like a colleague I used to have who worked children like adults. Don't blame him. You worked women like men before I began to caution you, didn't you? Anyway, don't do what he did. Do not rush everything with a children's choir. Go at it quite slowly. Let them play. In fact, become a child yourself. They'll love you. I always keep a candy jar close. Rewards! They love it.

When it comes to the singing, though, run only the melody. Children are active. They pick many things up at once, like a sponge. Therefore, make certain that even your piano accompaniment throughout the preliminary rehearsals is the main melody in unison. Even if you are running a two-part children's choir, it is advisable to begin with the melody. Once it sinks in, they are yours for the asking. You'll find that some of their brains run absolute pitch. You'll be the happier for it.

For what it's worth, it's good to keep an eye open for prodigies. So if I were you, I'd never keep children's work limited to singing. Start an instrument course, something sufficient to help them play tunes in a short time. Don't dare their attention span. It's not so long. Remain result-oriented. You see why you should have started on an instrument yourself? Let the children play recorders or violins or even piano. If you encourage rhythmic instruments too much, your emphasis in favour of definite pitch might suffer. So strike a balance with a bias for pitch over rhythm when it comes to musical instruments. It pays.

May wisdom flow into your heart for running your choir each day you stand to do so. May you find grace to work well with the fairer gender that makes your group tick so vibrantly. May you light up the path of young talents, transforming them into generals by a stroke of genius through your poor powers. May an issue of healing flow out of the music of your choir, bringing healing to the ailing, snatching the dying from the griping claws of death, and blasting the breath of rejuvenating life to the distraught souls of men, women, and children across the world.

*   *   *

Now that you are a better choirmaster, please reach me to share how this book has been of help to you or for any advice for that matter. I'm not just another busy author. I want to be your friend.

If you have bought this book and need any of our services, you qualify for a discount. Visit my training outfit's website. Just let me know.

For all your choir training needs, please visit www.tinglescroll.org; then reach me with your decision. The training would still be tailored to your choir's peculiar needs. What I'll be bringing is more than twenty years of experience with all kinds of choirs across choristers and musicians of various cultures across the globe. I'll be waiting to hear from you.

Now get in there and direct that choir!

Author Biography

For two decades, self-trained Soji Ojeniyi has led vocal groups of varying strengths across denominations, schools, and communities. He teaches *piano, voice, theory of music, history of music, history of jazz,* and *musical form* in schools and colleges of music. He presents candidates for the graded examinations of the prestigious Associated Board of the Royal Schools of Music, London.

He is the author of *Man Trust Thy Symphony, Star of Wonder,* and *All in Africa.* His works live on ezinearticles.com include *Music the Stimulant, Lad Alone, The Learning School,* and *Death Dealt Deadly.*

About the Book

If you have not worked effectively with a choir of one hundred voices or haven't been equally successful leading a choir of ten, you need to read this book. If you inherited a choir that is not quite in shape, whose music has no form, where rules are non-existent, and choristers are tone-deaf, please hurry and turn the pages.

From the music that moves the people to the love that binds or tears them apart, *Now That You Are Choirmaster* covers copyright to songwriting, funding to financial impropriety, part leading to verbal attacks, and fraternal fluxes to funny friendships.

www.ingramcontent.com/pod-product-compliance
Lightning Source LLC
Chambersburg PA
CBHW050414290526
45786CB00003B/1262